An American Rabbi in Korea

JUDAIC STUDIES SERIES

Leon J. Weinberger

General Editor

An American Rabbi in Korea

A Chaplain's Journey in the Forgotten War

MILTON J. ROSEN
Translated and edited by Stanley R. Rosen

THE UNIVERSITY OF ALABAMA PRESS
Tuscaloosa

The University of Alabama Press
Tuscaloosa, Alabama 35487-0380
uapress.ua.edu

Hardcover edition published 2004.
Paperback edition published 2018.
eBook edition published 2009.

Typeface: AGaramond

Cover design: David Nees

Paperback ISBN: 978-0-8173-5922-5
eBook ISBN: 978-0-8173-8226-1

A previous edition of this book has been catalogued by the Library of Congress as follows:

Library of Congress Cataloging-in-Publication Data
Rosen, Milton J. (Milton Jehiel), 1906–1976.
An American rabbi in Korea : a chaplain's journey in the forgotten war / Milton J. Rosen ; translated and edited by Stanley R. Rosen.
p. cm. — (Judaic studies series)
Articles translated from Yiddish.
Includes bibliographical references and index.
ISBN 0-8173-1400-8 (cloth : alk. paper) 1. Rosen, Milton J. (Milton Jehiel), 1906–1976. 2. Rabbis—United States—Biography. 3. Chaplains, Military—United States—Biography. 4. Korean War, 1950–1953—Chaplains—United States—Biography. 5. Korean War, 1950–1953—Personal narratives, Jewish. 6. Korean War, 1950–1953. I. Rosen, Stanley R. (Stanley Russell), 1931– II. Title. III. Series.
BM755.R5455A3 2004
951.904'27—dc22 2003027670

To my father
Rabbi Milton J. Rosen
of blessed memory

Contents

Illustrations ix

Maps xi

Acknowledgments xiii

Prologue xv

Prelude 1

1. The Chaplain 10
2. *Der Morgen Zhornal* 13
3. Invasion 15
4. *Der Morgen Zhornal* Articles December 4–December 25, 1950 25
5. Disaster and Retreat 39
6. *Der Morgen Zhornal* Articles December 28, 1950–January 14, 1951 41
7. Pusan Again 65
8. *Der Morgen Zhornal* Articles January 16, 1951–March 11, 1951 67
9. Japan Again 113

Epilogue 117

Bibliography 121

Index 123

Illustrations

Chaplain Milton J. Rosen, Japan, 1948 61

Chaplain Rosen alighting from transport, on one of his trips to military units in Japan, circa 1948 62

Chaplain Rosen with member of Tokyo Jewish Community before Jewish Chapel Center, 1949 62

Chaplain Rosen officiating at bar mitzvah ceremony of young member of Tokyo Jewish Community 63

Chaplain Rosen blowing traditional ram's horn, marking the High Holy Days, at the Jewish Chapel Center, Yokohama Command 63

Bon voyage to Chaplain Rosen, from many Japanese friends, returning to the United States from first tour of duty, summer of 1950 64

Editor Stanley Rosen, on Passover leave, with father, Chaplain Rosen, at Seder in Japan, 1954 64

Letter from the Japanese 116

Maps

Korea, Spring 1950 xviii

Invasion, June 25, 1950 16

North Korean Offensive, June 29 to September 14, 1950 21

U.N. Counterattack, September 15 to November 24, 1950 23

Chinese Attacks, U.N. Retreat and Evacuation, December 1950 37

Schematic of Chaplain Rosen's transport to and from the Battlefield, November 10 to December 31, 1950 59

Cease-Fire Line 119

Acknowledgments

My sincere thanks to Judith Higgins, Sandy Beddor, and Bonnie Hammond for their invaluable technical assistance in assembling this work and to my stepmother, Zella Rosen, of blessed memory, who generously provided precious photos, articles, and memorabilia from her personal collection. I also wish to express my special gratitude to my wife Bernice, who inspired and supported this effort.

Prologue

My father's correspondence from Korea during the conflict there gave little insight into the breadth and depth of his experiences. We knew that he had been serving in the area of the Chinese Communist intervention in North Korea in the winter of 1950, with the resultant encirclement and retreat of Allied forces. We knew that he had been evacuated with the other troops, by ship, and we noted, with some concern, that he had injured his foot while debarking. We were relieved that he appeared to be out of immediate danger and looked forward to his next correspondence. We had no idea that he was recording a sensitive, personal journal of the tragedy of that war from his unique perspective as an Orthodox Jew and dedicated Army chaplain. Among the family members, we vaguely remember that he mentioned once or twice, in a most casual manner, that he had written some articles in Yiddish for the New York Yiddish daily, *Der Morgen Zhornal,* (in English, the *Jewish Morning Journal,* also called the *Jewish Journal and Daily News*). He never mentioned a specific number of articles, nor, to my knowledge did he ever have a collection of copies. None of us ever saw any of them.

A few years ago, perhaps on the anniversary of his passing some twenty-five years before, during a conversation with my wife about his life and interests, the subject came up again, as it did from time to time within the family. On this occasion, my wife remarked on the irony of a situation in which everyone in the closer family spoke of the articles with a sense of regret and loss, but no one had done anything about it. While pointing out that one factor inhibiting a search was that the *Morning Journal* had not been published for years, I realized that that hardly constituted an insurmountable obstacle. Accordingly, I undertook an Internet search for institutions, such as theological schools, which might have records of Yiddish publications in their archives. To my surprise and delight, I was able to arrange for archives of *Der Morgen Zhornal,* recorded on microfilm, to be made available at my local library, through the generosity of the American Jewish Periodical Center. I then began the tedious process of viewing the newspaper, page by page, starting with mid-1950. In this undertaking, I was somewhat handicapped by the less than optimal quality of the microfilming and by the fact that I did not know when the articles had begun and how many I should be seeking. Finally, after several days of viewing, I recognized my father's name on the first of his articles, which he had written on November 10, 1950. The articles had been printed as they were received, which, considering the circumstances of war, could not be predicted. I therefore had to scan every page with care, until it finally became apparent that there would be no more articles after March 11, 1951. There was a total of nineteen.

After having translated the fine Yiddish of the first articles and sharing them with my wife, it became evident to both of us that this unusual collection of observations and word pictures, which could only have been composed by one with my father's unique background, deserved to be shared with others. While realizing that there are those who might have been able to translate the Yiddish with greater ease, I undertook this work as a labor of love, determined to reproduce his writing in English with scrupulous attention to the integrity of his words, his style and his nuance, so that the translation reads as he would have spoken. I have, therefore, edited only sparingly, in particular, where the difference in idiom in the two languages would need to be considered.

It was never intended that this work add to or substitute in any way for the extensive literature on Korea, Japan, and the Korean War. The summaries of the history preceding the Korean conflict, the war itself, and inferences regarding Korean and Japanese life and culture are included only to offer background enhancement for the articles and for the personality of their author.

The articles speak for themselves. I offer no further comment in this regard except to say that from a reading of them there emerges not only the impression of a most astute and sympathetic observer and participant, but also that of a heroic, patriotic, middle-aged man, without military training, who shared some of the usual gripes of the soldier, but who never complained about doing his duty, wherever that would be.

An American Rabbi in Korea

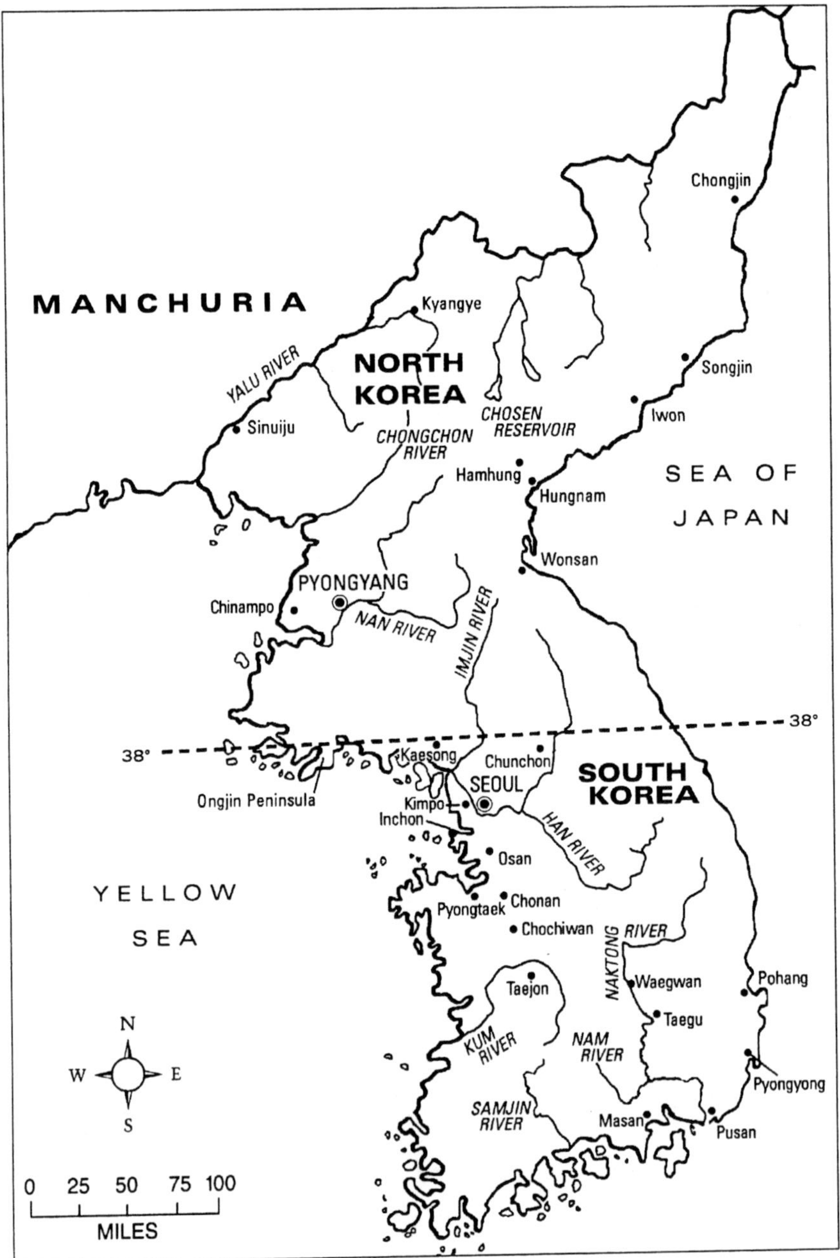

Korea, Spring 1950.

Prelude

Dipping into the waters defined by the Yellow Sea on the west and the Sea of Japan on the east rises the troubled peninsula of Korea. Its land mass borders China, Manchuria, and Russia and faces, across a small expanse of sea, a historic nemesis, Japan. Its tumultuous, largely Chinese dominated history spans at least twenty-five hundred years, approximately the last two centuries of which encompass uninvited contact with such western powers as Russia, Germany, Great Britain, and the United States.

Prior to the summer of 1950, however, it is doubtful if more than a minute percentage of Americans were conscious of Korea's existence. Under the suzerainty of the Empire of Japan from 1910 to 1945, during which all vestiges of Korean national identity were brutally suppressed, it was treated as a colony, the sole purpose of which was to provide support for the Japanese economy and, ultimately, for the Japanese military machine. Yet it was not regarded as a major military base during World War II, either by the Japanese or the Allies. It was not situated among the fortified islands that constituted the roadways of Allied conquest on the path to the mainland of Japan, thus escaping the notice of some of the more avid followers of the wartime geography of the Pacific.

In 1943, however, when the tides of World War II evinced hopeful surges in favor of the Allies, certain major heads of state began to consider the disposition of the postwar world. The first official probes in this regard were inaugurated in late 1943 at the Cairo Conference, when the United States, Great Britain, and China (under Chiang Kai-shek) took up the issue of postliberation Korea as part of the agenda. Representing the United States and Great Britain were Franklin Roosevelt and Winston Churchill, respectively.

The composition of participants in this conference provides a view into some of the unfounded assumptions under which it labored. One of the most important of these was related to the issue of the present and future geopolitical role of China and Chiang Kai-shek. China was still, at that time, to be the principal player around which postwar U.S. Asia policy would revolve. Although the Kuomintang government under Chiang was weak and corrupt, expending its limited resources in an ongoing struggle against the Chinese Communists rather than against the Japanese for much of the war, it was Roosevelt's hope that China's status quo could be strengthened by the incorporation of Russia into a postwar cooperative structure. In Roosevelt's view, the presence of Russia would work to dampen any tendency to civil war between the Chinese Communists and Chiang. The China that emerged from this configuration would prove amenable to American interests and those of the formerly colonized nations of the region. On the background of this perspective, Korea was given the vague promise of independence "in due course."

During the crucial conference at Yalta, February 1945, attended by Roosevelt, Churchill, and Joseph Stalin, Roosevelt pursued his planned Far East policy by acquiring Stalin's agreement to enter the war against Japan. In return, there would be territorial concessions from Japan relating to Russian losses in the Russo-Japanese War of 1904, as well as rail and port concessions in Manchuria. In addition, Outer Mongolia would be recognized as independent of China. The benefit of Russia's entry into the war against Japan was likely of less intrinsic importance than the hope that Russian support for a Chinese Communist–driven civil war could be avoided following Japan's defeat. At Yalta, Stalin agreed in principle to a four-power trusteeship in Korea, consisting of the United States, Great Britain, the Republic of China, and the Soviet Union, but it was not promulgated at that conference. Indeed, at the Potsdam Conference in July of 1945, although it was declared that the intent of the Cairo conferees to establish the ultimate independence of Korea would be realized, a framework for accomplishing this was not firmly dealt with at that time either. President Roosevelt had died in the interim between the two meetings. President Harry Truman was now representing the United States and may well have had no knowledge of the previous understanding regarding Korea, except for the vague, written statement emanating from the earlier Cairo accord.

Change of leadership in the United States, however, was by no means the salient cause of the failure of Roosevelt's plan. The assumptions on which the plan was based were simply not to be supported by subsequent history. Even at Yalta it could be seen that Stalin's understanding of the political future of the eastern European countries liberated by the Soviet Union would differ considerably from that of the western powers. At Potsdam and thereafter, a clear view appeared of the ever-growing suspicion and mistrust of Soviet intentions that were to characterize the decades to come. Thus, the portion of the plan relating to Russian cooperation fell away. It might have been fair to expect of Roosevelt that he consider the possibility that Stalin could not be relied upon, but one would be hard put to demand that he foresee the tremendous upheaval in China, which would inevitably frustrate the Asian portion of his proposed policy.

The role of China in this equation may reasonably be understood as a consequence of the historic involvement of two men, Chiang Kai-shek and Mao Tse-tung. In 1911, Sun Yat-sen, the great hero of modern China, led a successful revolution against the Manchu dynasty, opening the way to the establishment of a republic. The creation of the Marxist model of government in Russia, as a result of the turbulent years of revolution and early consolidation by the Bolsheviks from 1917 through 1922, fortuitously presented Sun with convenient alternatives in postrevolutionary government. In the 1920s, Sun's Nationalist Party, the Kuomintang, largely organized and promoted under Sun's trusted lieutenant Chiang Kai-shek, held parts of Southeast China, but felt the need to expand northward against the warlords of that region. The small Communist Party, including among its members Mao Tse-tung, was involved in this and other ventures.

Following the death of Sun Yat-sen in 1925, the era of cooperation between the Chinese Communists and the Kuomintang began its destructive dissolution, primarily at the aggressive instigation of Chiang, who, in 1927, betrayed his Communist allies following the joint capture of Shang-hai. In the wake of an unprovoked massacre of three hundred Communists in that city by troops of the Kuomintang, the deliberate, experimental character of the Sun Yat-sen–led revolution was forever altered. The Russian mentors disappeared, and the remaining Chinese Communists fled to Kiangsi province, in southeast China, where Mao Tse-tung was soon recognized as their leader. Chiang sent multiple forces to wipe out Mao's troops, but none was successful.

In spite of the aggressive intrusion into Manchuria by the Japanese in 1931,

Chiang persisted, in a manner characteristic of his policy for nearly two decades, to ignore the outrageousness and ominous portent of the Japanese invasion, and concentrated all his military efforts against the Communists. The latter, for their part, had grown significantly in number during the few years following their flight from Shang-hai and were able to defend themselves in large, bloody battles against the Kuomintang in spite of meager resources. Ultimately, however, they were trapped in the area of the town of Juichin, from which, in 1934, Mao and his close companions and fellow leaders Chou En-lai and Chu Te broke out and led some ten thousand followers on the historic, six-thousand-mile "long march" to Yenan, in Shensi province. With the exception of a relatively short period of time, from approximately 1937 to 1938, during which there was a measure of unity against the Japanese invasion of China proper, the tragic story of modern China is told against the background of the titanic battle of the corrupt but more traditional Kuomintang against the ever more powerful, but equally autocratic, peasant-based regime of the Chinese Communists.

The Communists waged a relentless guerrilla war against the advancing Japanese, retreating when strategically advantageous, returning when the enemy moved on. They proved to be a constant thorn in the flesh of the Japanese Army and a continuing provocation to the suspicious Chiang. Simultaneously, they pressed an eminently effective recruitment campaign and introduced land and rent reform in the areas under their control. A vicious campaign of destruction and intimidation in Communist-held territory by the Japanese in the early 1940s succeeded only in increasing hatred of the invaders and enhancing Communist recruitment. Chiang's unending efforts to squeeze Mao's forces into an ever-tighter death grip also failed, in the long run. In 1944, the Communists broke out of a trap in Shensi to which Chiang had committed large numbers of troops. These troops might have been better employed in opposition to the ominously aggressive Japanese offensive south of the Yangtze River at that time. That offensive, which resulted in the destruction of an important network of American built and operated airfields, might under the appropriate circumstances have led, ironically, to a reasonable facsimile of Roosevelt's intended China policy, since it inaugurated a new American diplomacy toward the Communists. This diplomacy conceived a policy of providing arms to the Communists, advocating joint efforts with the Nationalists and considering a coalition government, which, if it had come about, could have had a profound effect on subsequent history.

Indeed, early contacts by a delegation from the United States achieved encouraging signs from Mao that a good working relationship between him and the United States was possible and desirable. Mao appeared ready to cooperate with the Americans in joint efforts against the Japanese on Chinese soil and to maintain a positive relationship in the aftermath of the war. Mao and the representative of the United States signed a paper proposing a Chinese government in which the Kuomintang and the Chinese Communists could preside jointly. It was rejected by Chiang, however, forcing an uncertain American policy to manifest its ultimate bias. Although the United States continued to encourage an end to the civil war and urged cooperation between the two sides, eventually sending the highly regarded General George C. Marshall to mediate, it never abandoned Chiang Kai-shek, nor did it successfully rein him in. Chiang never relinquished his violent quest for total power in China until he was finally defeated by Mao in 1949, fleeing with his remaining troops and functionaries to Taiwan.

Thus, as a result of Chiang's obsessive, ruinous drive to reign over all of China, despite ample evidence of the lack of unified support on the part of his devastated and tortured people, and further, because of the American government's failure to offer consistent, convincing assurance of good will and support to the reality of Mao's position among his countrymen, Roosevelt's dream was forever shattered. Moreover, the formidable enemy, which Communist China was to become in such a strikingly short period of time, would be the source of tragic consequences for the Americans and Koreans.

The lack of a definitive mutual understanding between the Soviet Union and the United States regarding the fate of a liberated Korea opened the way for disastrously divergent interpretations of the Cairo agreements, so casually reaffirmed at Potsdam. It was Truman's intent to establish military control, in association with taking the Japanese surrender, to be followed by a period of United Nations supervision, leading to the development of a democratically constituted, independent state. A detailed program, with logistics, does not seem to have been an integral part of this policy, however, unlike, as it later became evident, the case with the Russian approach. The Americans were overwhelmingly preoccupied with the defeat of Japan in the late summer of 1945. The first atomic bomb was dropped on Hiroshima on August 6, followed only a few days later by the second, on Nagasaki. The Soviets, true to their pledge at Potsdam, declared war on Japan on August 8, entered Manchuria on August 9, and swept into North Korea by August 10. The Japanese surrendered on August 14. Included in the terms was the arrangement for the Soviets to take the surrender in the north of Korea and the Americans in the south.

By August 25, the Russian Twenty-fifth Army, already ensconced in Pyongyang, had set up a "People's Executive Committee," with handpicked officials, some of whom had been prepared as a Korean political cadre well before being returned to Korea by the Russians, and others of whom were Korean soldiers, who had also been trained in the Soviet Union. Thus, when the 38th parallel was chosen by the Americans as a convenient dividing line for the acceptance of the Japanese surrender, nearly a month before the first American troops appeared in Korea, the Russians had the capacity to establish a Soviet-style communist government in North Korea.

In the south, Lieutenant General John R. Hodge arrived on September 8, 1945, from Okinawa, commanding some fifty thousand men. It was his job to take the Japanese surrender south of the 38th parallel and to maintain order, while establishing some form of interim governing arrangement. The latter was to serve until trusteeship or a U.N.-sponsored plan for ultimate (but not immediate) independent statehood could be created. The assumption of the U.S. government was that the Koreans, who had been permitted no significant political or bureaucratic participation in governmental activity under the Japanese and little general involvement in Korean political affairs prior to Japanese hegemony, would not possess the experience or maturity in governance necessary to promote and maintain an independent national sovereignty. Indeed, for a time, Hodge employed Japanese officials and military, as well as some equally despised minor Korean bureaucrats, in their old positions, to the dismay of the Korean citizens. The latter had a very different view of the realities on the ground, in the aftermath of the war. They had expected immediate independence and had no understanding of the need for paternalistic monitoring and guidance, in spite of the total physical, economic, and political shambles they had inherited from their Japanese captors. Indeed, a remarkable number of political entities proclaiming themselves to be appropriate leaders of a new, independent Korea sprang up, some even before the actual surrender of the Japanese.

One such party, the Korean People's Republic, was of considerable size and had constructed a proposed governmental apparatus presumed capable of taking immediate control of Korean affairs. This entity received no such recognition by General Hodge, nor did any others, in those early days. The issue of power in South Korea needed to be associated not with numbers alone, but also with credible leadership, a quality deemed to be sorely lacking in any recognizable form. Into this vacuum came the highly controversial Syngman Rhee, a lifelong advocate of an independent Korea, living most of his life in exile, and long the head of a group of expatriate Koreans who regarded themselves as a provisional Korean government. Brought back by Hodge in the hope of providing a leader around whom the Koreans could rally, Rhee proved a most difficult ally, condemning in the fieriest terms any deviation from immediate independence under his autocratic rule.

The turmoil, which characterized the political scene in South Korea at that time, was exacerbated following the meeting of the Council of Foreign Ministers, representing the United States, Great Britain, and the Soviet Union, in Moscow, in December of 1945. At this meeting, a trusteeship for Korea, lasting up to five years, was proposed and adopted. The South Koreans, with the exception of the Communist-controlled organizations, who were, apparently, acting in concert with the North Korean Communists, reacted strongly. This was a time of much anti-American feeling, with seething guerrilla activity and political agitation, creating the necessity for riot control and other repressive measures. The milder response of the South Korean Communists appears to have worked to enhance the position of the Russians at a joint panel meeting in March of 1946, at which the Russians demanded that only those who had not acted in opposition to the Moscow accords regarding trusteeship could participate in the discussions. The Americans rejected this since it would have meant that all discourse over the issues would be held only with Communists.

The commission dealing with the issue of trusteeship met again in the summer of 1947, but again, achieved nothing. Truman, desiring to eliminate the heavy burden of occupying Korea, with no immediate resolution of the current problems in sight, took the matter to the United Nations for the purpose of setting up elections in Korea for the establishment of an independent state. The elections were meant to affect all of Korea, and the state was meant to represent a government for the entire country. The U.N. Temporary Commission was not allowed to enter North Korea, however, thus rendering impossible a nationwide election. The elections were held, nevertheless, in the south, with a massive voter turnout. Rhee and his supporters won a majority in the new National Assembly, in the spring of 1948. A constitution was promulgated in the summer of that year, and Rhee was elected president. De facto, he was president of South Korea, only. The Americans, with worldwide military, political, and economic pressures, especially in Europe, where the aggressive, repressive nature of Communist policy and intent was now abundantly clear, and with the reality of vastly diminished postwar military resources at hand, began implementing a withdrawal of troops from South Korea. This was complete by the summer of 1949. They would leave behind considerable stocks of light weapons and equipment and a five-hundred-man military assistance corps.

During these tumultuous three years, developments in the north proceeded with deliberation and speed to consolidate the early and all-encompassing power of the Communist state, under Kim Il Sung, a Korean who had spent the war years with a Communist guerrilla organization, said to have fought the Japanese in Manchuria. He had come back to Korea with the Russians and had been strongly supported as a suitable leader for the evolving Communist regime in North Korea. Arriving in North Korea in October of 1945, heralded as a hero, he was placed on a fast track to political prominence by the Russians. By 1946, he had become chairman of the Interim People's Committee, which carried out Soviet policy in North Korea, including land reform and party legislation. He soon became prominent in a new legislative body called the Supreme People's Assembly, which, in 1948, established a constitution, ratified in early September 1948. On September 9, 1948, at Pyongyang, the Democratic People's Republic of Korea was announced. Kim Il Sung was its premier.

Both North and South Korea had begun building small constabulary units by 1946, which ultimately expanded to army units. From the start, however, American policy, on the background of the unstable civil and political situation in South Korea, on the basis of the overriding U.S. world strategy, and in the wake of the strident bellicosity of Syngman Rhee, was ambivalent. On the one hand, the United States had not supported the South Koreans since the end of World War II only to leave them totally defenseless before the Communists in the north. On the other hand, the Americans were not enthusiastic about being drawn into war by virtue of Syngman Rhee's desire to incorporate all of Korea under his leadership. Accordingly, he was given weapons and promises of military aid in the future but was not supplied with the means to carry out offensive operations. Indeed, the state of preparedness of the South Korean military, both in terms of training and equipment, at the time of the withdrawal of the U.S. troops in 1949, was less than optimal.

Russian policy was constrained by no such ambivalence. The power over the people of North Korea was absolute, and the actions of the North Korean national government were reflective of Russian Communist policy. When the Russians withdrew the main bulk of their forces from North Korea in 1948, leaving behind only small contingents of trainers and advisors, the Korean People's Army was well on the way to its optimal strength. In June of 1950, it would stand at least 150,000 well-trained and equipped fighting men, thousands of whom had been trained in the USSR and China, with heavy armor and a functioning air force. The South Koreans had less than 100,000 fighting men, equipped and prepared as indicated. The stage was set.

I

The Chaplain

Milton J. Rosen was born in Vilna, Lithuania (then under Russian domination), in 1906, the youngest of six children. His family immigrated to the United States shortly afterward, settling in Chicago, where the elder siblings rapidly adjusted to their new surroundings. This easy adjustment proved less a source of blessing than a cause of distress to his father, a man of deep piety and Jewish identity who feared his older children were bound for religious assimilation and determined that his youngest son would avoid that fate.

Accordingly, Milton's father took his wife and young Milton to Palestine, settling in Jerusalem where Milton studied Torah and Talmud and absorbed tradition. The ominous rumblings of World War I were approaching, however, when Shabsai Rosen succumbed to pneumonia, leaving his wife and son to face the years of war alone together, with no escape possible.

His mother, too, soon became ill and passed away. Milton was taken in by the well-known Diskin Orphanage in Jerusalem where he survived the war and attained great scholarship in Jewish studies. At the close of the war, with the help of Chief Rabbi Kook and his family in America, he returned to Chicago. He was fourteen years old.

Following a year in elementary school, during which he added English to his knowledge of Hebrew, Yiddish, Aramaic, and Arabic and passed through the standard curriculum, he entered Harrison High School in Chicago, graduating in 1926. Concurrently with his secular studies, he was enrolled at the Hebrew Pre-Theological College of Chicago, graduating in 1925. From 1925 to 1929, he studied at the Hebrew Theological College of Chicago, where he was ordained as rabbi in 1929. He later acquired a B.A. degree in philosophy from the University of Wisconsin, Madison.

Milton married Sarah Rosen in 1929, before taking his first rabbinical position in Dayton, Ohio. They had two children, Stanley (Hebrew name Shabsai, after his grandfather), and Carol Betty (Hebrew name Chaya Basha, after her grandmother). He was a practicing Orthodox pulpit rabbi for nearly nineteen years before entering the United States Army chaplaincy late in 1947. His entrance into military service from his last pulpit, in Madison, Wisconsin, seems to have occurred in a rather informal manner, as he received orders to report to Fort Bragg, North Carolina, to take up his duties as a chaplain without any preliminary instruction. In his words: "I bought an officer's uniform. I then went up to an Army headquarters in my vicinity and asked them to teach me how to put on my tie correctly and how to pin my rank and chaplain's insignia in the proper manner. I then received a ten-minute lesson in the science of proper saluting. With that, I parted with my life as a civilian rabbi and proceeded by railroad to my assigned post at Fort Bragg."

At Fort Bragg he was able to continue his education as an effective officer and chaplain through the excellent tutelage of his well-versed chaplain's assistant, rapidly becoming adept at writing orders, requests, and reports. He was regarded on post as an experienced old-timer. No one ever learned that he had not attended Chaplain School. The failure to be indoctrinated into a particular mode of behavior or attitude with respect to the chaplaincy, however, may well have worked in his favor. He simply carried on being a rabbi, ministering to his military charges in the same active manner he had practiced with his civilian congregationalists, teaching, leading services, and counseling. He incorporated Jewish civilians from nearby communities into his Sabbath and holiday services, and they extended their hospitality to the soldiers, providing refreshments, a homey atmosphere, and warm social contact. His lectures were open to all, a practice that would be maintained in Japan, to which he was soon assigned, arriving in Yokohama in January 1948.

Under the firm but benign rule of the U.S. occupation, the Japan to which Chaplain Rosen was assigned in 1948 was remarkably improved over that of the devastated, starvation-ridden Japan that had surrendered in the summer of 1945. Already, numerous reforms had been enacted and put into effect by the new, bicameral Diet, under the recently written and adopted constitution, officially promulgated in mid-1947. These measures included land reform, political rights, social progress (encompassing the expansion of women's rights), and substantial alterations in economic practices, such as the curbing of the power of the great monopolies and the development of organized labor. American assistance had largely removed any traces of hunger in the population, and an ever increasing return to normal agricultural and industrial activity left the Japanese poised for the soon to be realized years of economic wonder.

Chaplain Rosen plunged into this atmosphere of resurgent, spiraling energy with enthusiasm, creating an uncommon tour of duty marked by intense activity on behalf of the spiritual needs of his military congregants and, in addition, by a unique outreach to the civilian Russian and German Jews who had landed in Japan as refugees from Nazi Germany. Beyond that, he opened the doors of his chapel, the first distinctly Jewish chapel in Army history, to the Japanese public. Here they could join the soldiers and other members in the enjoyment of the social events and cultural offerings, as well as the ever-present kosher refreshments and informal mingling.

He traveled all over Japan to offer religious services and instruction to the troops under his official jurisdiction. He spoke, often, to Japanese audiences interested in knowing more about the religion and fascinated by the chaplain's obvious knowledge of the cultures and philosophies of the East. This knowledge was part of a study he undertook, along with that of the Japanese language, soon after his arrival in the country. The Japanese eventually established an organization to explore the world of Judaism, seeking information and guidance in study, as well as formal lectures, from Chaplain Rosen. When his tour of duty came to its end in the summer of 1950, he was given a lavish farewell banquet by the Japan-Israel Society, which owed its inspiration and existence to his leadership. He was seen off by hundreds of military, civilian and Japanese friends, before he embarked for the United States.

Meanwhile, the churning magma beneath the Korean volcano was no longer to be contained, and, on June 25, 1950, North Korean troops, tanks, and air units inaugurated a massive invasion of South Korea. Chaplain Rosen was on the high seas, bound for America, when the news was announced aboard ship. Some feared the ship might turn around. It did not. For Chaplain Rosen, however, the time at home would be very short.

2

Der Morgen Zhornal

Der Morgen Zhornal, known in English as the *Jewish Morning Journal,* and later, as the *Jewish Journal and Daily News,* was established in 1901 in New York, and for a time was the only morning Yiddish newspaper. Early in the century, it took over the editorial and classified advertisement departments of the previously prominent *Tageblat* (*Daily Bulletin*), and shared its orthodox philosophy. Its principal competition was provided by the two other prominent dailies, *Der Tog* (*The Day*), started around the onset of World War I in New York City, and the well-known *Forverts* (*Forward*), also published in New York from 1897.

The *Jewish Morning Journal* shared in the surge of popularity and circulation increase enjoyed by the Jewish newspapers in the first decades of the twentieth century, when the emigration of Yiddish speaking, socially and politically aware refugees from the harsh conditions and persecutions of Eastern Europe filled the east coast of America with great, and as yet nonintegrated, cultural energy. In addition to acquiring a reputation for gathering the largest amount of current news, the paper also offered the Yiddish reading public the popular cultural fare that enriched the lives of the aspiring immigrants. This included biographies, novels, political and social explorations, and literary comment. Serialization of literature was not an uncommon practice among the Yiddish papers, and such intermittent reports as those sent by Chaplain Rosen, in later times, were well received.

The *Jewish Morning Journal* merged with *The Day* in 1953 and continued to publish until 1971, when demand for Yiddish publications in general reached a nadir. At its height, it had a circulation of over 110,000. At the time of its closing, the figure was considered closer to 50,000. In 1914, virtually every Jew in the larger cities of the East spoke Yiddish. In 1930, there were still over 600,000 Yiddish speakers in New York. The end of the great immigrations and the successful integration of the masses of newcomers into American society ultimately dampened the drive to maintain a separate language of social comfort. At the time Chaplain Rosen's articles were written, however, there was still an avid audience for his observations in Yiddish.

3

Invasion

Already in the spring of 1950, there were intelligence reports coming to the Far East Command in Tokyo regarding major troop concentrations north of the 38th parallel in Korea and evacuation of civilians from that area. For a considerable period of time prior to these reports, there had been border clashes between forces of the North and South Korean armies, which appear to have been seen as sources of tension rather than immediate concern. They seem to have been evaluated on the background of current Weltpolitik, rather than on the actualities on the ground. Seen from the perspective of North Korea acting as a puppet of Soviet international policy, intelligence analysis in Tokyo did not indicate that this was a convenient time for an aggressive move against the South. Thus, no alarm was raised. Indeed, on June 25, 1950, a large number of the armed forces of the Republic of Korea (ROK) were on weekend leave, most of the important officials in Washington were out of the city, and General Douglas MacArthur was incredulous when the North Korea People's Army crossed into South Korea.

The attack occurred all along the waist of the peninsula, with the main assault carried out by two infantry divisions and an armored brigade. First, the Ongjin Peninsula in the west was hit. This was followed by strikes at Kaesong, which stood before the capital, Seoul, and soon thereafter by aggressive moves farther to the east, at Chunchon. Seoul was being attacked almost simultaneously by air. The ROK army was represented by only four regiments on the line at the onset of the thrusts, and although there was a brief attempt at counterattack by the ROK Seventh Division, the latter was, as was to hap-

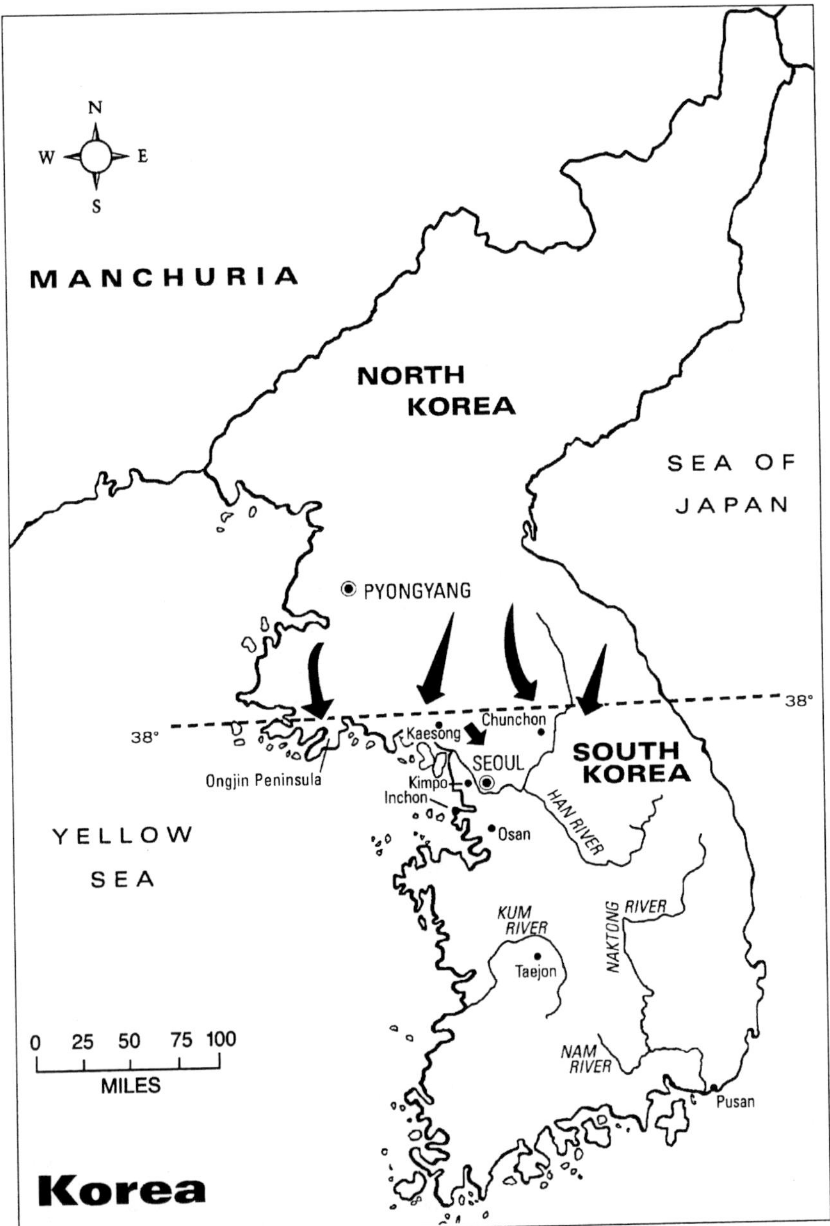

Invasion, June 25, 1950.

pen all too often in this conflict, soon left vulnerable by the collapse of its flanking division, forcing it to withdraw. This left the way open to Seoul, which finally fell to the enemy on the fourth day of the invasion. There was tremendous confusion and disarray in Seoul. Members of the Korean Military Advisory Group (KMAG) evacuated, as did thousands of others, but ultimately, the bridges across the Han River below Seoul were blown, taking hundreds of Koreans to oblivion and leaving thousands stranded on the north side.

Although having failed to anticipate the attack, the government of the United States, in spite of the poor state of military preparedness in which it had left the South Koreans on its original withdrawal, did not intend to preside over the demise of the new state. Aside from the moral issue, it was considered imperative that the leader of the democracies of the world draw a line against what was regarded as pure, international Communist imperialism, albeit with the keen recognition that if the Soviet Union challenged this decision militarily, there could be a most unpleasant consequence. The Soviets had by no means followed the example of the West in a frantic demobilization after World War II and would not even lag in nuclear war technology for long. Nevertheless, the United States, with the Soviet Union boycotting the U.N. Security Council, acquired from the United Nations two resolutions supporting immediate intervention. The first, on June 25, called for the withdrawal of North Korean troops from South Korea. The second, on June 27, asked for the members of the United Nations to aid the South Koreans in their defense against the aggression from the North. This effectively placed the prosecution of the military effort under the leadership of the United States.

The first active response was to send immediate aid to the South Koreans in the form of military supplies and equipment, without the dispatch of combat troops. The rapidity with which this was recognized as totally inadequate reflects the combination of skepticism relative to the capabilities of the South Korean units on their own and cognizance of the actual menace of the swiftly advancing North Koreans. Particularly effective on behalf of the enemy was his armor. The Russian T-34 tanks were a terrifying weapon in the eyes of the South Koreans and, indeed, in the view of the first American troops to face them in Korea, for there were no comparable tanks available to them at the time with which to counter them. The U.N. side did not even have effective antitank weapons.

By June 30, it was abundantly clear that not only active participation by air and naval units of the U.N. Command, but also rapid deployment of ground troops was urgent. The president of the United States turned to the Far East Command, where General MacArthur had at his disposal four understrength, underequipped, and underprepared divisions, under the command of Lieutenant General Walton Walker, chief of the U.S. Eighth Army. The Twenty-fourth Division was the first American unit to deploy in strength on the peninsula. This division was under the command of General William F. Dean, who sent an advance force to Pusan, in southeast Korea on July 1, under Lieutenant Colonel Charles B. Smith. Task Force Smith, as it became known, arrived at Taejon, midway between the 38th parallel and Pusan on July 2, consisting of less than five hundred men.

They were sent north to Osan, about midway between Kaesong and Taejon, in the hope they could halt the advance of the relentless North Koreans, giving more time to build up the presence of the Twenty-fourth Division and other arriving units, at Pusan. The task force was deployed along the road into the town, armed with some artillery and some bazookas, presumably prepared to engage the enemy. Although they were somewhat effective against the North Korean Infantry, the latter were preceded and supported by units of tanks that were virtually impervious to American weaponry, which was inappropriate and insufficient against them.

Task Force Smith fought vigorously but was defeated and scattered. Although the remnants attempted to reassemble in the next few days, the defense of Osan was no longer an option. South Korean units attempted to hold back the progressive southward advance of the North Koreans, trying to provide time and space for the Twenty-fourth Division, now moving up to face the onslaught. Elements of the Twenty-fourth, however, now headquartered at Taejon, were pushed back ever southward and eastward, as they retreated at Pyongtaek and Chonan, falling back to the Kum River line, the last barrier before Taejon. The Americans had not yet found the solution to the enemy tactics, which were repeated consistently. It was a process in which an advance force of tanks would push through the defense lines, undaunted by impotent artillery, followed by well-trained and determined infantry. Some of these would stream around the flanks to join the tanks, which now, in concert with the troops before and behind the Allied soldiers, would destroy all efforts at unified resistance.

While the arrival of heavier tanks on the U.N. side, able to destroy the T-34's, would, in the near future, help to balance the North Korean advantage in armor, the U.N. forces, primarily American and South Korean at this time, provided a rather inconsistent and unreliable defensive posture. The South Koreans were in large measure undertrained, led, for the most part, by an officer corps of privileged and often corrupt appointees, and the Americans were, to a painful degree, garrison soldiers, accustomed to the easy life in Japan, often not even trained as infantry. The result was a situation in which officers could set up a good plan of action and deploy troops appropriately, only to learn that large gaps in the line occurred, as a result of wholesale abandonment of positions by fleeing troops.

When General Walker arrived in Pusan on July 13, taking over command as head of the Eighth Army, he brought with him units of the Twenty-fifth Infantry and First Cavalry Divisions, but by July 15, the Kum River line had been breached, and Taejon lay open. This was disaster. It is, perhaps, indicative of the desperation of the situation, that in the midst of defeat and retreat, a cause for celebration could be found in the arrival of weapons to which Russian tanks could be vulnerable. "General Dean tried to hold the enemy at Taejon for a couple of days. The enemy came in force, capturing Taejon, destroying the Division, and capturing General Dean. But one thing had been accomplished; a T-34 tank had been destroyed, which boosted morale. The 3.5 inch rocket launchers had been arriving in Korea, and they could stop the T-34 tanks."[1]

Toward the end of July, the U.N. forces were faced with extinction on the ground or a retreat into the sea. At least five regular North Korean Divisions, the Second, Third, Fourth, Fifth, and Sixth, as well as the 105th Armored Division, were variably or simultaneously squeezing the U.N. troops into an ever smaller, semicircular perimeter on the southeast coast. Against these ever aggressive salients, which were driven by a powerful need to drive the U.N. forces off the peninsula before they could gather sufficient strength to prevail, were the exhausted Twenty-fourth and the Twenty-fifth and elements of the First Cavalry Division, as well as the newly arriving First Provisional Marine Brigade and the Fifth Regimental Combat Team. There were also five South Korean Divisions. These defensive forces were strung out along a front that left their defenses very thin. Time, however, as the North Koreans knew all too well, was on the side of the Allies.

As the fighting continued into August, the conflict lost none of its ferocity, but the perimeter held. The U.N. forces were building up more personnel and weaponry, including more effective armor, and maintained unquestionable air superiority and virtually unopposed sea-lanes and naval support. By September, the force of the offensive against the perimeter began to wane. The North Koreans had taken terrible casualties and were now significantly outnumbered, their supply lines had been overstretched and battered ceaselessly, and they were about to be squeezed into a trap.

On September 15, 1950, in a controversial and technically difficult move, General Edmond Almond, commanding X Corps, a combination of the First Marine Division and the Seventh Infantry Division, carried out the long-considered plan of General MacArthur to land forces at Inchon, just to the southwest of Seoul. Encumbered by numerous islands at the entry to the harbor, a configuration of an outer and inner harbor, and an extraordinary range of tide and current aberrancies, the success of the operation was particularly remarkable. More to the point, it was extremely effective, allowing for the rapid retaking of Seoul and bringing pressure on the North Koreans, still fighting in southeast Korea at the perimeter, to begin their inevitable withdrawal northward. The withdrawal turned into a general rout, with pursuing American troops often overrunning the fleeing North Koreans. The confusion notwithstanding, The U.N. units steadily pushed northward, and then, on September 26, linked up with elements of X Corps, which had landed at Inchon.

With the military initiative and momentum now in the hands of the U.N. forces, the issue at the beginning of October was, "What now?" They could stop at the 38th, achieving a return to the status quo ante. They could cross the 38th and advance to a point approximately midway between the 38th and the Yalu River, effectively aborting the power of the North Korean state. Or they could continue on to the Yalu and unify the country. Already there were indirect threats emanating from China that the advance of American forces across the 38th would bring about the intervention of Chinese troops. The warning did not apply to South Korean soldiers. The tendency of the American leaders was to consider this a bluff, although it will be noted that they became more and more cautious as the Allies moved closer to Manchuria. For the time being, however, the ominous buildup of Chinese units over the border in Manchuria appeared to be ignored.

South Korea's I Corps crossed the 38th on October 1, moving rapidly up the eastern section of North Korea. Before long, there was a broad front advancing north, with U.S. I Corps, South Korea's II Corps, and their ROK First

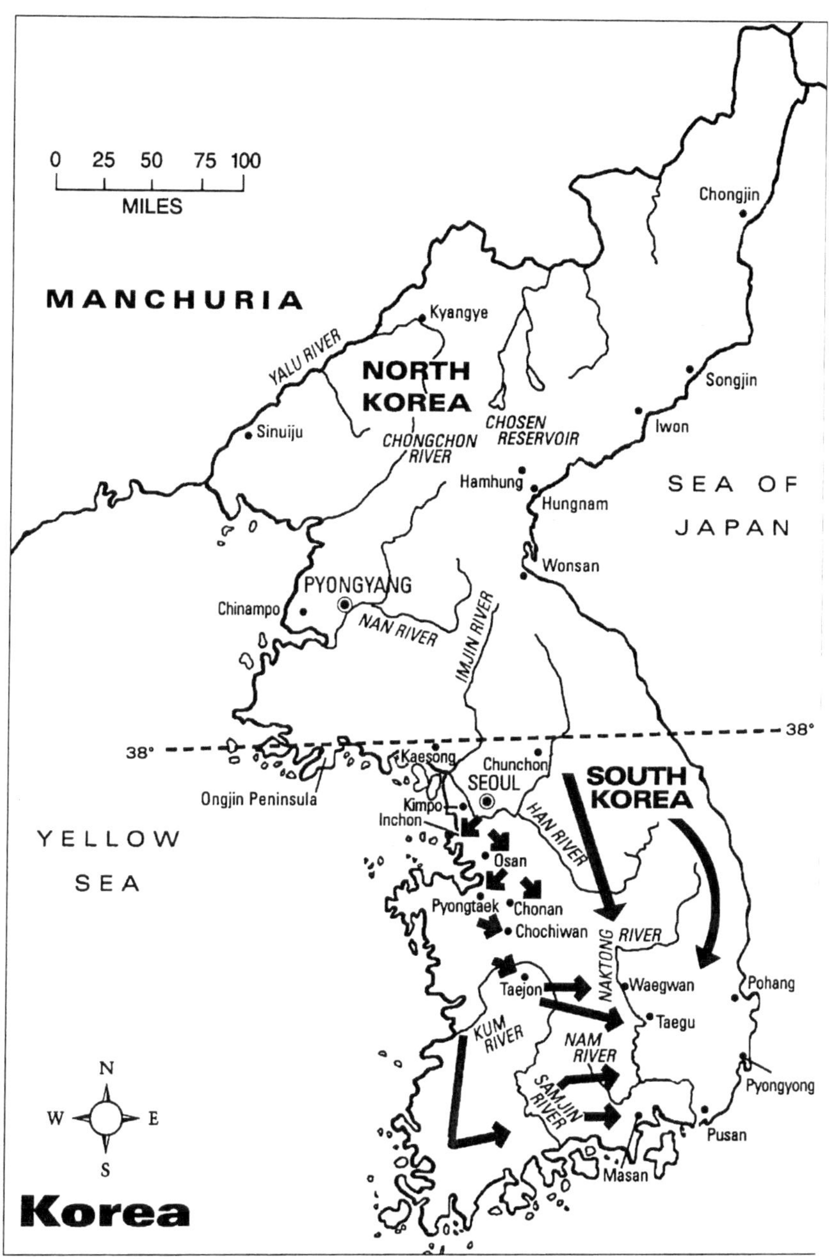

North Korean Offensive, June 29 to September 14, 1950.

Division, among others, pressing the North Koreans toward Pyongyang, as well as centrally and eastward.

Meanwhile, General MacArthur, for reasons of his own, directed General Almond to move his X Corps to the port of Wonsan, on the southeast coast of North Korea. The First Marines went by ship from Inchon around the peninsula, ultimately debarking at Wonsan. The Seventh Division traveled by rail to Pusan, thence by ship to Iwon and later, to Hungnam, both ports lying north of Wonsan.

On October 15, 1950, the famous meeting between President Truman and General MacArthur took place on Wake Island. It was during this meeting that the president was assured that in the unlikely event of Chinese intervention in Korea there would be the "greatest slaughter." By October 20, the North Korean capital of Pyongyang was securely in Allied hands. U.N. forces had reached the Chongchon River in the west. The U.S. Marines were in Wonsan on the east coast. Elements of the Seventh Division were north of them in Iwon, and the ROK I Corps was driving ever higher on the northeast coast.

A U.N. resolution of October 7 had called for a plan of reunification of the peninsula, with the establishment of appropriate political institutions, and ultimate withdrawal. The manner and timing of these events were left vague. The U.S. Joint Chiefs of Staff were also less than precise in their interpretation of this mandate but appeared to favor caution with respect to any provocation of the Chinese. It was considered prudent that any significant advance to the area of the Yalu River be undertaken by ROK troops only.

The Joint Chiefs were somewhat taken aback, therefore, when, on October 24, 1950, General MacArthur ordered his entire command to advance to the Yalu River. For various reasons, the Chiefs took no action relative to this move. General MacArthur was the commander on the spot, and he had authored the brilliant success at Inchon. Besides, following the Chinese threat of intervention, nothing further had been heard from them. Where, after all, were the Chinese? The chilling answer, which the Joint Chiefs of Staff and MacArthur were to learn all too soon, was that they were in North Korea, hundreds of thousands of them. They had been infiltrating silently, at night, in the mountains of North Korea, in part through the gap between the U.N. forces on the left and those on the right, for weeks.

The ROK Sixth, part of the central west push of the ROK II Corps, which had pushed beyond flank protection on its way to the Yalu, was attacked and decimated. American and South Korean elements of the Eighth Army were

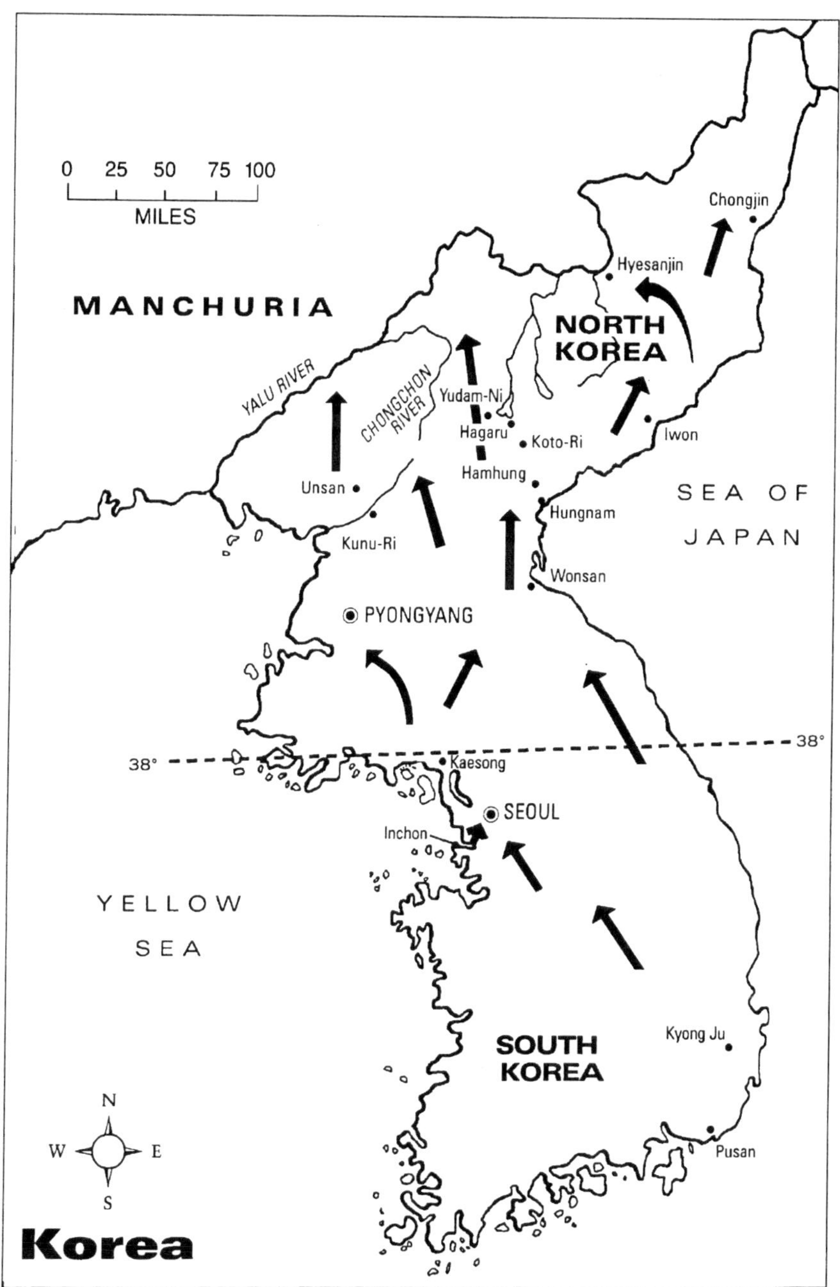

U.N. Counterattack, September 15 to November 24, 1950.

attacked and pushed back at Unsan. Units sent to open an escape path for encircled U.N. troops were ambushed and severely reduced. At the same time, as if none of this were happening, General Almond's X Corps continued its advance to the North. The Marines headed up into the area of the Chosen Reservoir, soldiers of the Seventh Division left Iwon to drive toward the Yalu, and the South Koreans kept pushing northeast.

Then, suddenly, the Chinese disappeared. Puzzlement gradually gave way to confidence. Perhaps this was not a serious threat. There seemed to be no large-scale follow-up. November began to pass without further evidence of Chinese involvement. The Americans celebrated Thanksgiving in an optimistic mood. American soldiers arriving in South Korea in early November do not appear to have been oriented to the imminent threat of significant Chinese opposition. It was at this point in the war that Chaplain Rosen debarked at Inchon.

Having been in the States only a very short time following his tour of duty in Japan, Chaplain Rosen had been sent back to Japan, apparently in October 1950, uncertain as to his ultimate duty post. By early November, however, it was clear that he would be sent to Korea. It is not evident from notes or any other source when he engaged to write of his experiences as army chaplain on duty in the Far East, but his first articles, written in Yiddish for the popular New York Yiddish newspaper, *Der Morgen Zhornal,* appeared in December, with a lag time of approximately three weeks. Thus, when he was describing his arrival in Inchon and the subsequent transport by rail to the port of Pusan, he was writing in November, with the information and assumptions available to him and the rest of the troops at that time, but by the time the first article was published, the headlines of the newspaper were already telling a different story. As his first article appeared, the headlines were relating the retreat by U.N. soldiers from the North Korean capital. His second article was written sometime in mid-November, but was not published until December 18, when the headlines announced the pressure of Chinese attacks in the area on the east coast of North Korea, from which American forces would be evacuated, in the face of the Chinese onslaught. By the time he wrote his third article, about the first of December, the evacuation had begun, and the editors had not heard of his status for some time.

Note

1. Jeffrey Solomon Rosen, *The Korean War* (unpublished manuscript, 1975).

4

Der Morgen Zhornal Articles December 4–December 25, 1950

Der Morgen Zhornal, December 4, 1950

In a Military Camp in Korea, Destroyed by the Communists

by Chaplain Milton J. Rosen

On the 5th of November, on a mild, early Sunday morning, we left the harbor of Yokohama on the ship *General Hasse.*[1] The ship carried more than a thousand officers and soldiers. By Tuesday, November 7th, we entered the Harbor of Sasebo, in southern Japan. There, another thousand passengers boarded, before we sailed off on a tranquil sea, arriving at the Korean Harbor of Inchon on the 10th of November.

This was the very same port that had been invaded by the Americans on September 15, as a result of which the armies of North Korea had been entrapped. The invasion had opened the way to Seoul and the later breakthrough to the 38th parallel.

It is characteristic of this harbor that no ship can anchor close to shore. Small boats are the only means of effecting a landing, and the success of the latter depends on the weather and the water level. If one misses the opportune tide at which the water level is optimal, he must wait until the early morning hours to try again.

This was precisely our situation. We had arrived well past the optimal time and were forced to debark from the ship into small boats before dawn. One can imagine the scene—a harbor in which from 3:00 a.m. to 11:00 a.m., eight hours, countless small boats were transporting great numbers of men, packed like herring. The debarkation was made more arduous on an individual level by the necessity to descend from the ship carrying heavy baggage on the shoulders. Clambering down the ladders required acrobatic skill.

As it happened, I was on the last boat to leave the ship, a circumstance that really made it nearly impossible to make landfall, as the water level had dropped very low. It continued to drop, and we noted muddy strips of land appearing far from the shore. Having no choice, we turned the boat to the side, floating into a small channel, where the water had not yet run off. Hungry and tired, we got out onto a small wooden bridge. Since 2:00 a.m., when we had been awakened, we had had nothing to eat.

On land, masses of Koreans awaited us, ready to carry our heavy packs to the trucks and land wagons. We had assembled at a point near the vehicles that were to transport us to our temporary quarters. We smoked cigarettes, took a breath and looked around, wondering where we were. It was a clear, warm day. I observed the destruction of the large buildings, wrought by the bombardment of the American war ships. Hardly a brick lay atop of another. Day and night, the Koreans cleared the road of the rubble. I looked at the faces of the hundreds of Koreans, men, women, and children, walking the streets. They wear long, white kaftans, white as shrouds. The elders, with white beards, appear patriarchal, the simple masses, to the contrary, ragged and remote. The women, their hair scrupulously combed, also wear white garments, rather than the kimonos worn by the Japanese. They all seem to have dark faces and sad eyes. One can see in their eyes the pain of their suffering and poverty. But behind the superficial characteristics, one perceives a pride, a sense of self worth, of one who faces you without fear or shame. I offered them cigarettes. They accepted the gift, but they did not bow humbly, as do the Japanese. They remained standing. They thank you with a nod of the head and a polite smile.

Our train consisted of a chain of cars that in the States would be used only for horses and cows. The soldiers filled the cars. The cars smelled, and they shook so violently, we held on, to avoid falling out of the open doors. I had never seen such a decrepit locomotive. Perhaps, I thought, this was a version of the earlier, more primitive engines used during the Russo-Japanese war, in Korea.

It was now after 2:00 p.m., and we still had not had a bite to eat. We drank water and smoked cigarettes, to drive away the hunger. Our train was covered overhead by an armada of aircraft, which had been accompanying us the entire way. We appreciated the protection. Although we were armed with rifles and pistols, we knew that guerrilla bands inhabiting the mountains could suddenly attack. The aircraft were our guardian angels.

The train moved slowly past the outskirts of Inchon. Along the way, hundreds of people greeted us with waves of their hands. They wished us luck in the war, which we conduct to bring them freedom. The soldiers threw candy and cigarettes through the windows. We passed the straw roofed huts. Amidst the dirt and squalor, which struck our eyes as we passed, there stood a handsome woman, well dressed, smiling and waving to us from her well-kept balcony.

We arrived at our camp, some six miles from Inchon, where we waited wearily through the long roll call of officers and men. Apparently no one was missing. By 4:00 p.m., we were quartered in the well-constructed buildings set up by the Americans before they left Korea several years earlier. The barracks had contained all the usual modern amenities, but when the North Koreans broke through, they wrought destruction throughout the housing. At the time of the current American invasion landing, the North Koreans took off with whatever they could move, before they left, including the pipes, the mirrors, the beds, the windowpanes, door windows, and toilet seats. They left only the bathtubs.

We were lodged in these barracks temporarily, pending our orders for transportation to our various destinations. We had no beds, but the Koreans brought us straw mattresses. We were ordered to spray them with DDT, to ward off myriad crawling things. We had no sheets or blankets, but every soldier had his sleeping bag, the blanket-lined sack into which one crawled to sleep. Among the military, discussion continues as to whether it provides a soldier sufficient warmth.

"Thank God," I thought, "the hunger comes to an end," when, at pitch dark, we were called to eat. We stood in line with our mess kits, inching forward to the food pot. I arrived at the desired spot to find, to my considerable disappointment, that what was being offered was pork, which of course, is not to be eaten by a Jewish chaplain. I had to be content with vegetables, fruit, and coffee.

The camp had been open for only three weeks, in the process of rebuilding. Hundreds of Koreans, men and women, old and young, were involved in the reconstruction. The camp was to be transformed into a military center for the midportion of Korea.

By 9:00 p.m., we were preparing ourselves to sleep on the floor. I did not feel sleepy, nor did the hard floor and the cold walls beckon me to slumber. I noticed several "houseboys" talking in the corner of the room, and I felt a desire to participate in their conversation. I asked them if they speak Japanese, and receiving an affirmative reply, I tried to communicate with them in my weak Japanese. I spoke to them of my experiences in Japan, and they opened their hearts to me. One of them, a handsome, well built young man, told me that before the war he had been a student at the University of Seoul. He had studied philosophy and was an admirer of John Dewey and American psychologists. I told them I am a Jewish chaplain, and they informed me that they knew a lot about Jews. They knew Jewish history and were aware of the suffering of the Jews through the many generations. Finally, they expressed great interest in the new State of Israel.

I perceived they knew many facts about Israel, but they wanted more information from me. They were strongly interested in the development of Israel. Israel was an independent land. Will Korea also realize salvation? The most voluble student said openly that everyone knew very well their hope lay only in the U.N. The terrible conditions behind the iron curtain were no longer a secret.

I offered them cigarettes, bade them a good night and went back to my room, where there were mattresses for eleven men. No one could sleep. They talked about the war and about the coming march to the fronts. One officer had orders for North Korea on the morrow, in the area of battle. This was to be his second trip to the front. Not too long before, he had taken a bullet at the battle of the Naktong River. He had been hospitalized in Japan. Now he is being sent back to the same company. He expressed his fear. Would he remain alive through a second time? His fellow officers tried to console him. God had protected him the first time. He would do so again.

Officers, enlisted men, all lay on the floor, their eyes open. They spoke of their wives and their children. They hoped for a miracle—that the war would suddenly end. They exchanged opinions, actually questions. Is the war necessary? How long will it last? Eternal questions regarding the futility of war. Each tried to quiet the other with words of reassurance, but in the heart of every man there was a great fear, an unbridled terror of tomorrow.

Der Morgen Zhornal, December 18, 1950

With the American Military Forces on the Way to the Battlefront in Korea

by Chaplain Milton J. Rosen

I have been in Korea since the 10th of November and am still underway. The station to which I am supposed to be assigned is Wonsan, where I am to become a member of Headquarters, Tenth Corps, under the command of General Almond. That I can't get there at the appointed time is due to the transportation problem. Virtually all our ships, aircraft, and trucks are dedicated to one task: the urgent conveyance of essential war material and ammunition to appropriate areas near the battle lines in North Korea. It almost appears as if the weapons have taken on more importance than the men who must use them.

When we first arrived in Inchon Harbor, we learned that we must await a second ship, which was to carry us to Wonsan. Why the first ship carried us here and there along the coast of Japan, arriving finally at Inchon, only to leave us to the second ship to take us to Wonsan is a puzzle to us. Wags call it a military secret.

Now, after ten days, we receive the order to leave this place. We feel certain that we should travel directly to Wonsan, which is located on the northwest side of South Korea.[2] We pack up in great haste. Large trucks take us to the train station. It is 2:30 p.m. We wait at the battered depot. It is a cold Sunday afternoon. The soldiers are confident that we are finally on the way to our assigned station, Wonsan. The confidence wanes rapidly, however, for we are told that our destination is Pusan, which is in the opposite direction, at the southeastern coast of South Korea.[3] This was the point from which the Americans had launched their counteroffensive against North Korea.

This trip drags on with incredible slowness. The hours stretch out in burdensome fashion, and the cold days seem an eternity. It becomes colder minute by minute. Finally, a major drives up in a jeep. He makes a thorough inspection of the train and finds the cars so neglected that they are not suitable for animals. The filth is overwhelming, and odors are suffocating. The place is full of lice and human waste. The major makes no secret of his disgust with the station superintendent who has failed to realize that the American soldiers would be subject to infection with countless illnesses under such conditions. The station, however, is in total disorder. There is no one to order to clean the cars. The Korean officials pretend not to understand. On these half-destroyed, filthy trains, Korean refugees travel in great numbers, train after train, with their few possessions, an endless stream fleeing the North Koreans. They ask no questions. They establish themselves in the dirt and live like animals.

We wait long hours, without the slightest indication that we might expect a second train. Meanwhile, it grows dark. The cold becomes bitterer. We tear out strips of wood from the broken columns of the station. We start fires and warm ourselves around them. Each soldier takes out a can of rations, cooks supper, and eats with great appetite. Hundreds of Korean children, nearly naked, dirty, hungry, gather around us. They wait for us to throw away the empty cans, so they can use them for their meal. It is difficult to describe the terrible conditions of these unfortunate children who tremble with the cold and wait for the opportunity to lick the inside of a discarded tin can. These are small children with old faces, old from troubles, from hunger, and from the terror of war.

As we are finishing our supper around the fires, a train full of English soldiers arrives. They too had been required to take a second train and are to travel with us. They follow our example and make fires. As it turns out, they have had more experience with such situations and find nothing new or strange in them. They enjoy their rations, become cheerful, and sing songs. Their song drives away the gloom that has dominated us, amidst the rampant destruction in this strange and unfortunate land.[4]

Finally, we are shown the train that is to take us from here. At first sight, our hearts sink. It is a long train of boxcars. However, we make peace with our lot, if only we can now lay down our weary, tired out bodies. The soldiers, with their full packs, fill up the cars. Each car must accommodate thirty-three men. It has actually been calculated how much space each soldier needs to stretch out on the floor. Inside, soldiers are chopping wood for fires to keep them warm on the long ride to Pusan. The distance from Inchon to Pusan is only 350 miles, but the trip must take several days and nights. The war is flaring up in all directions. Guerrilla camps lie along the way. The reports of friendly and enemy fire are ominous and intermittent, and we do not feel too confident of the ancient rails and deep tunnels, either.

After sweeping away the dirt from the car floors, we set up our bedding.

Our lighting consists of several small candles. We spread out. It is cold, cramped, gloomy. One can hardly move a limb. Finally, with a whistle blow, the locomotive lurches from the spot. After we have traveled only ten minutes, several soldiers shoot through the openings into the air. This is apparently done to warn the enemy that we are prepared to repel a sudden attack. No one is fooled. Everyone knows the mountains are full of the enemy troops, which lie in wait. About ten thousand North Koreans are said to be in the area. Only a day earlier, the radio reported the guerrillas had entrapped about three hundred Americans, of whom more than twenty had been shot to death. One comes to the conclusion that the best medicine for fear is to go to sleep, but sleep does not come easily on this cold, hard floor. We lack blankets, and it takes a few hours before sleep finally envelops us and frees us from fear and worry.

The dawn appears early. The awakened soldiers are enthusiastically cooking up some coffee. The dirt around us had already invested our bodies, but we have no complaints. This is the life of a soldier in wartime. The important thing is that we are still alive. Let the train ride forever, as long as we do not hear the sound of weapons.

It may well be worth noting that most of these troops have been to the front before. Some of them have been wounded, some two or three times. They are just back from the hospitals, ready to rejoin their battalions and fight again. It is remarkable how easily they speak of their experiences in combat. One of them shows me two holes in his back, where a bullet entered one and exited the other. He wears the same shirt he wore when the holes were made. The wounds are still red, and yet he is ready to go into the fire again. Many soldiers express amazement at the rapid cure rate and modern methods of the military doctors. The latter appear able to resurrect severely wounded men in a matter of days.

In this manner, two days and nights pass, and the monotony seems to creep into our very bones. There appears to be no end to this journey. Only when the train pauses at a station does one feel alive again. Small, skinny children approach with all kinds of articles to sell. I have never in my life seen such energetic, ambitious businessmen as these Korean kids. They buy and sell nearly anything one can imagine. One kid, about thirteen years old or so, comes with a handful of money, asking to buy American cigarettes, candy, and chewing gum. He wants to buy a carton of cigarettes for twelve hundred won.

Twelve hundred won equals about three dollars American. Some of the soldiers take out stashed cartons of cigarettes and make some money for themselves. Chewing gum is also a precious article in Korea. Six hundred won, or a dollar and a half, is paid for a pack of gum, which costs a nickel in America. Nearby is another young man, a real salesman. He asks fifteen hundred won for a pack of cigarettes. It is a lively scene. There is noise and racket. There is buying and selling, and the merchants are young children with the appetites of real businessmen. These are Korean children who have no desire for a communistic regime. They are dying to be capitalists.

At one of the station stops, I crawl out of the car and try to move my benumbed feet. I note a man with a girl, standing against a wall, carrying on a pleasant conversation. I come up to them, and begin to speak to them in Japanese. Hearing that I speak Japanese, the man becomes quite friendly and joins me in a long conversation about the war. He tells me about his life, about how the North Koreans burnt his house and robbed his savings, how he was now returning to Taegu, his previous home, to see what remained for him and what he might do. His wife disappeared in the confusion of the war, and he is now left with his daughter. Suddenly he asks me about the insignia on my uniform. I explain that I am a Jewish chaplain. It turns out that I have once again encountered a Korean who is familiar with Jewish history. He is a Protestant and purports to know the role that Judaism plays in the world.

Although he is a friendly individual, I do not appreciate his remark that all Jews are rich. From what source does he get this? That is what he heard, he declares. A peculiar thing. I've heard the same remark from a number of Koreans whom I have met. I explain to him that this impression is a fable and falsehood engendered by anti-Semites. I start naming for him the best-known men of wealth, the millionaires of America, who are certainly not Jewish. His eyes began to open. Not only does he not know that Rockefeller is not Jewish, he does not even know that Truman is not Jewish. He, as so many thousands of his people, is convinced that all the leaders of America are full-fledged Jews.

Der Morgen Zhornal, December 25, 1950

Sent to the Front in Korea as Chinese Begin Offensive

by Chaplain Milton J. Rosen

Editors' note: the last news we had regarding Chaplain Milton J. Rosen was of his involvement in the Chinese trap at Chosen Reservoir in Korea. Chaplain Rosen, the spiritual leader of the Jewish soldiers in Korea, conducted religious services for the soldiers and Marines through the entire period of the bitter fight to break out of the encirclement and force a way through to the port of Hamhung. Chaplain Rosen had enough prayer books and prayer shawls to provide all the Jewish personnel with the means to chant their prayers, amidst very dangerous and uncertain battle conditions. We pray that Chaplain Rosen will be rescued from the trap and we hope to receive from him further, fascinating descriptions of his observations of the Korean War.

Pusan, December 1950

As our train, after a trip of several days, finally arrived in Pusan, I observed that this was probably the one train station in Korea that was not damaged in the battles. The depot building remained untouched. The rails were not smashed.

Behind the depot, large trucks awaited us to take us to our camp, which was located in a remote island in the area of Pusan. The only connection between this island and the city of Pusan is a bridge, which opens several times a day to allow the passage of large ships. When we arrived at the island, they placed us in a building that had served earlier as a school for Korean children. There was an array of military cots strewn about in considerable disorder. It took no longer than a few seconds for our American soldiers to appropriate these beds. The "houseboys," the Korean children, helped to arrange the bedding for the soldiers. I was struck by the manner in which these frail, skinny Korean youngsters carried on their bony shoulders the heavy mattresses and soldiers' duffle bags, which seemed to be three times the weight of their young bodies. Incidently, I learned later on, that as soon as a Korean child takes his first steps he is taught to bear the "yoke of life," and that this weight becomes greater every year as the child grows.

Also, the Koreans, men or women, are offended if you indicate the desire to help them carry their burden. The slim Korean woman is as strong as I am. She can carry a pack on her head, two packs in both hands, and a large pack on her shoulders, and, despite this, walks lithely, as would an acrobat.

We waited in Pusan more than a week for a ship to take us to Wonsan. I used the waiting time to acquaint myself a little with the life of the Koreans. Every evening I would leave the camp and go for a walk through the streets of Pusan. Here in the city one sees a mixture of the old and the new Korea. One sees the men and women either in the white, shroudlike garment or in modern clothing, but nearly all of them carry a package on their heads or shoulders. Among the passersby are old men, genuine elders, who carry on their shoulders a sort of wooden saddle, constructed like a stool. On this stool, they place a veritable house of furniture. The only help they have to maintain their balance is a long stick, which they carry in their right hands.

You would never see in the street a young girl speaking to a soldier. If you should stumble upon such a scene, you may be assured that the parties are brother and sister or man and wife. The concept of morality in Korea is much different than one would imagine from afar. One evening I was sitting in one of the dry goods stores, carrying on a conversation with a lovely sales clerk, who is unmarried. My knowledge of Japanese and my status as an American enabled me to carry on a discussion about the war and the troubles that Russia imposes upon the world, and thus, talking, eventually to divert the conversation to the subject of the relationships between men and women.

The saleslady, an unusual beauty, a tall, modest girl of twenty-three years, told me she fled from Seoul when the North Koreans captured the city, and now she works here in Pusan for her existence. Her rather weak knowledge of English suffices to help her communicate with the American soldiers who come here to shop. She told me her parents are still in Seoul. They seek a young man who would be suitable as a husband for her. She depends entirely on their choice, for she herself never comes into social contact with men.

The proprietor of the store, next to whom stood his wife, told me that fate permitted him the privilege to be with his bride before their wedding. He even had a chance to demonstrate his affection to a degree. Their adjacent porches bore swings, on which they would glide back and forth, casting longing eyes toward one another, expressing their love in silence. Fortunately, their modest courtship was rewarded, as their parents were in favor of the match. They are very happy with their two children.

He told me that the Communists shot hundreds of girls in Korea when it became known that the latter had fraternized with the American soldiers who had been stationed here several years before. Today, one can hardly see a young woman over twenty-five or twenty-six in Seoul or in Inchon, so many of these were killed.

Since I have been in Pusan, I have heard, regularly, wild tales concerning the fate of American soldiers captured by the North Koreans. It is said that those Americans who had had relations with Korean girls were emasculated. As for the girls, we have already spoken of their fate. These stories do not appear to be fanciful. The American soldiers are openly reluctant to have social relations with Korean girls. The fear of revenge weighs heavily on them.

The Koreans are not especially hospitable to strangers. They do not invite one to their home as do the Japanese. In general, they are not enthusiastic to mix with foreigners. To this day, many Koreans cannot forgive South Korean President Syngman Rhee for having married a Caucasian woman from Austria.

It is an irony that despite the strict moral barriers between men and women in this country it is a fact that homosexuality is widespread. A man dare not accost a girl in the street with an immoral suggestion, but it is common to see young men grabbing passersby and offering immoral acts. It is often dangerous to walk a dark street at night for fear of being attacked by hoodlums. The larger cities in Korea are poorly lighted. Even a city the size of Pusan impresses as dark, and the kerosene lamp is more common than the electric light.

The Koreans have a reputation of being talented thieves. They are extraordinary experts at their work. One could have a thousand eyes and still be robbed. I, myself, was relieved of my money several times, when walking the street at night. The Korean houseboys are accused daily of theft by the camp soldiers. They steal money, documents, handkerchiefs and socks, shoes and underwear, and because these thefts occur so often, we do not trust even the honest among them. It is, however, appropriate to mention that we have no lack of takers among our young men, and not seldom have I been called upon to give moral counsel to certain American soldiers who have unlawfully acquired various things from the Koreans. Once, while out for a walk, I encountered a soldier with a splendid wristwatch, and I asked him how much he had paid for it. He answered quite innocently that he had picked it up in a jewelry store and did not find it necessary to pay for it. I gave him a firm lecture on honesty, on the spot, but this is only a minor example of the pretty deeds some of our soldiers are capable of doing. It is a discouraging experience to walk into stores in which are sold blankets, field jackets, and various items of military equipment, which can come only from our camps. When the responsible individuals are brought before the commanders, they blame the Koreans for their own thefts.

The streets of Pusan, especially the streets in the area of the train station, are always packed with troops, wearing the uniforms and speaking the languages of various lands and folk. There is a babel of people and tongues, Americans, British, Indians, Canadians, Koreans. It seems the nations of the world march by us.

The most attractive impression is made by the Indian soldiers, with their well-combed beards and sharply pressed uniforms. Observing this parade of the many and varied troops, one gets the sense that the world actually means, once and for all, to defeat those who provoke wars and seek to destroy our world. One considers the phenomenon of these soldiers of diverse lands, marching peacefully together over the streets as brothers, having the common purpose and will to paralyze those dark forces that would drive the earth to ruin. Indeed, one takes comfort from this international military spectacle on the streets of Pusan, and the hope for a better, more beautiful world grows stronger.

For eight days I had had the opportunity to study Korean life closely. On the ninth day, I received the order to leave Pusan. Our entire unit was carried by trucks to the port. There, LSTs awaited us. These are small Japanese boats, constructed especially for the transport of weapons, tanks, trucks, and heavy artillery. The belly of the boat appears to open hastily and swallow up all the waiting material with great rapidity. It is also used to carry troops when a quick landing is in order. As it turned out, there were only two officers in our boat, I and one other, among the hundreds of soldiers who filled every corner of the craft. Because we were only two officers, we were able to be quartered in well appointed, comfortable quarters.

As soon as we had arranged ourselves in our cabins, we heard the sudden news over the radio that a new battle was beginning, with the Chinese. The announcement arrived like thunder in the heavens. We were, indeed, sailing north, where the battle had broken out. We knew then that our original destination had been altered. We would not go to Wonsan. We would go to Hungnam. The latter is over sixty miles north of Wonsan. I knew now I would be the Jewish chaplain closest to the front. The news was not appe-

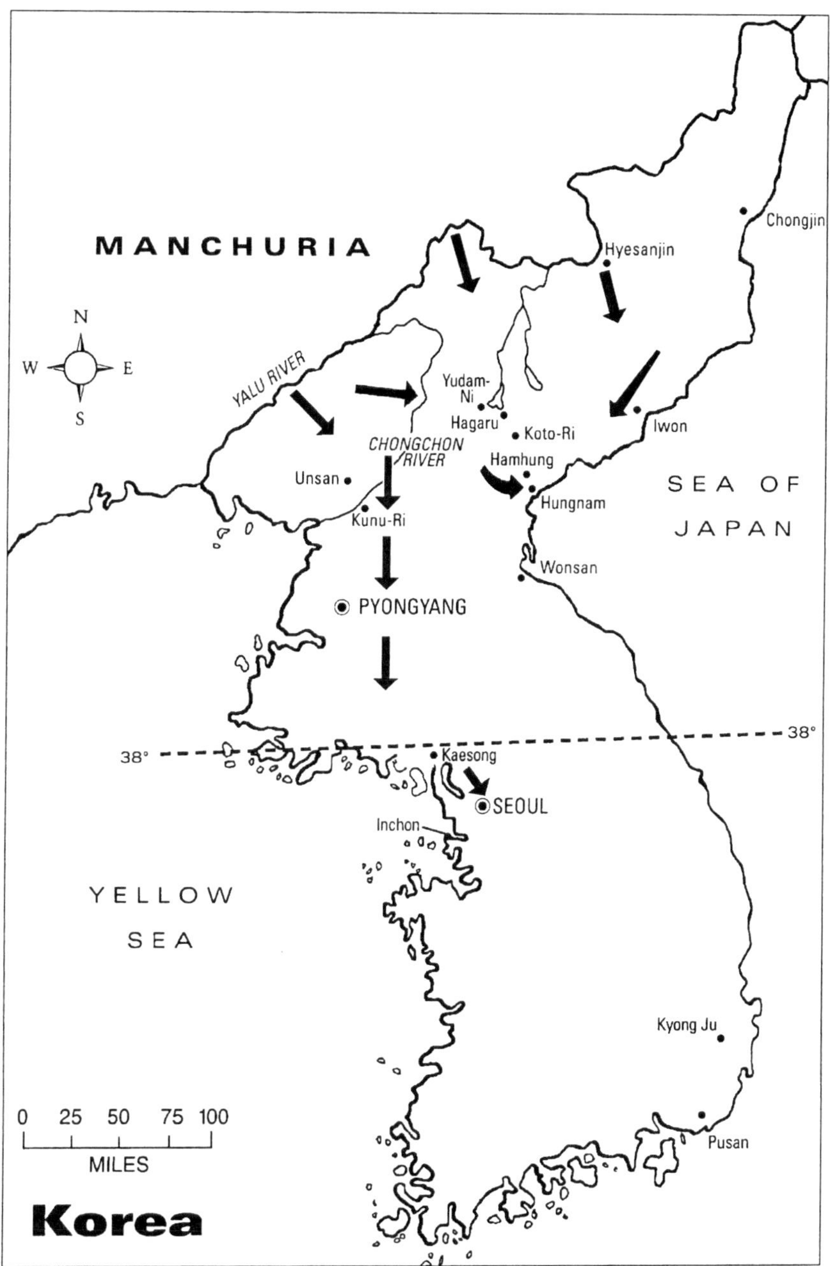

Chinese Attacks, U.N. Retreat and Evacuation, December 1950.

tizing, especially since the announcement came one day after General MacArthur had told us we were soon to go home.

Notes

1. Spelling uncertain; transliterated from Yiddish.

2. Likely, this is a misreading on the part of the *Morning Journal;* Chaplain Rosen was obviously familiar with his destination, which was on the southeast coast of North Korea.

3. This was indeed the situation. Rather than return by ship, around the western side of the peninsula, to the northeast side, the troops went across the country by rail, to the southeastern port, Pusan. From Pusan, they were transported northward by ship to the southeastern coast of North Korea.

4. The British and Commonwealth troops played an enormously important part in the Allied effort to stabilize the front and thereafter to drive back the enemy to positions along the 38th parallel, which the North Koreans had violated.

5

Disaster and Retreat

On November 25, the Chinese reemerged in great force and with great fury. They rapidly destroyed the ROK II Corps, driving them back with such speed as to leave the U.S. Second Infantry Division without a right flank, while the ROK First Division was being hit on the Second's west. Efforts to reinforce the retreating troops from around Kunu-ri failed. Indeed, Kunu-ri, just east of the Chongchon River, was bypassed by the Chinese, who not only continued southward behind U.N. forces, but also ambushed some seven thousand retreating soldiers of the Second Infantry Division, south of the city. Only four thousand emerged from the trap, the survivors being indebted to fierce intervention by the American Air Force and by the British Commonwealth troops, who fought northward to open the road. The entire line withdrew southward, and by December 5, General Walker's Eighth Army was positioned below the North Korean capital of Pyongyang. Within a few weeks, the Eighth Army would be back at the 38th parallel and would not be able to stop there. Meanwhile, General Almond's X Corps was beginning to react to the reality of their situation, after an apparent reluctance to recognize that they were now on the defensive. Even as late as November 27, the First Marines were being urged to advance northwest in an aggressive fashion, as if the momentum had not been altered. On the 28th, however, the Marines to the west of the Chosen Reservoir and the units of the Seventh Infantry Division to the east were being vigorously attacked by up to six Chinese divisions. From Yudam-ni to Koto-ri, on the way toward Hamhung, the Americans were surrounded and pummeled. Heroic efforts were made to assemble the remnants of the Marines from Yudam-ni and the soldiers from the eastern portion of the Reservoir at Hagaru. Only a portion of the troops made it to Hagaru, from which Marine General Oliver Smith led all who had made it to that point on an extraordinary fifteen-mile journey in bitter cold, fighting all the way, until, after nearly two weeks, they were able to gain access to Hamhung, and thence, to Hungnam and evacuation. Meanwhile, the ROK and other Seventh Division elements, which had been extended up toward the Yalu, had been withdrawn to the port area around the time General Smith's ordeal was beginning.

Evacuation of U.N. forces took place almost simultaneously on the west and east coasts of North Korea during December and early January, in a masterful performance by the Allied navies. On the west, at Chinampo, in North Korea, and at Inchon, in South Korea, enormous amounts of equipment were salvaged, in addition to the successful removal of some seventy thousand individuals. This was accomplished under difficult circumstances relative to the port conditions, but under somewhat less immediate pressure from the enemy. On the east coast, the pressure against Hamhung continued throughout the month of December. While the Marines were evacuated by the middle of the month, followed by ROK troops, the Army units remained a bit longer, while tens of thousands of Koreans were taken aboard as refugees. The last Army units did not leave Hungnam until Christmas Eve. It seems Chaplain Rosen was among the latter. He appears to have spent close to a month in the Hamhung-Hungnam sector, until the end of the American presence in North Korea, writing extensively of his experiences during that time.

6

Der Morgen Zhornal Articles December 28, 1950–January 14, 1951

Der Morgen Zhornal, December 28, 1950

In a Hospital for Wounded American Soldiers in Korea

by Chaplain Milton J. Rosen

It was the first of December, when our small Japanese boat, packed with soldiers and transporting guns, brought us, with considerable difficulty, into the harbor not far from the city of Hamhung. The frost burned our faces. It had snowed all morning without cease. The gray sky, full of clouds, appeared to merge with the very ground over which the military port sprawled.

No sooner had we arrived at the harbor than fantastic rumors began to circulate regarding the great victories of the Chinese armies, which were attacking not far from our area. A Japanese passenger aboard my boat told me, in a tremulous voice, that as early as dawn, he had picked up on the radio a report that President Truman had threatened to drop the atom bomb on the Chinese if they did not withdraw their armies from Korea.

This is not pleasant news. The heart beats a little faster. The head feels as if it were spinning on little wheels. Everyone is overcome with a sense of insecurity. One tries to escape the feeling of panic. When the soldiers look across the harbor to the tall, immense mountains before them, however, it is difficult not to think of the large groups of enemy camps that lie hidden there. No one wishes to kid himself about the danger that threatens on all sides.

Before long, the open trucks, covered with wet snow, take us into Hamhung, a town about twelve miles from the harbor. Constantly, along the way, we see hundreds of Korean men, women, and children, loaded with their luggage and household treasures on their shoulders and heads, wandering somewhere, to far places, to hide from this new enemy. These itinerant Koreans know exactly, as well as we, how great is the imminent hazard. And so, pervaded by concern and vague expectations, we arrive, after a short ride, to Hamhung, and we stand before the headquarters of Tenth Corps. I meet my commanding chaplain in his office. He greets me very warmly, but, at the same time, informs me that today or tomorrow we may yet have to return to Hungnam, to the port town from which we had just now come. The situation is bad. The enemy moves ever nearer, and the best defense line will be the area closest to the sea. The chaplain, Colonel Toby, warns me it would be best not even to unpack. The order to withdraw could come at any moment. Hastily, I take out only the most necessary articles of clothing and go to my quarters for the night.

The room is cold, cheerless. Several sleeping officers share the space. I am less fortunate then they, however, as they possess beds. I am forced to arrange my bedding on the floor. Actually, I am rather accustomed to this by now. For not less than the last six weeks, I have usually slept on the floor, no mattress, no pillow, no warm blankets.

The first night's sleep is an uneasy one for all of us. I am up early in the morning to visit the hospital, which is fairly far from the city. My jeep brings me directly to the entrance, where I observe immediately the naked picture of this terrible war. One after the other arrive the ambulances and Red Cross trucks, packed with wounded soldiers.

I soberly gaze at the damaged bodies, which are being carried from the ambulances, and shudder. They carry out young boys with bloody wounds on their heads and faces and other parts of their bodies. I see, also, a whole row of frozen men, brought by air, direct from the battlefield. Many could not be brought out in time, and they simply froze to death. A hospital doctor told me that about eleven hundred soldiers had been brought here in the course of half a day. Not far from the hospital lies the cemetery, where new graves are dug daily. The area of the cemetery grows larger every day, and the wounded men can see through the hospital windows, as each new grave is prepared. I am unable to understand how an architect could plan a cemetery directly opposite the hospital. Such an architect must have been the servant of the devil.

I find no Jewish personnel among the wounded. I acquire the hospital list and learn that three Jewish doctors and two assistants work there. Then, as I am continuing my inspection in the hospital, word comes suddenly that the place must be made ready quickly for the Seventh Division, which is already retreating from the battlefield. This means that what we have expected has happened. Wherever one looks, one sees large trucks with military equipment moving on Hungnam. All is carried out hastily and in a proper manner. Every branch of Tenth Corps withdraws according to its established order. Our group will withdraw Sunday afternoon. Everything in our office is already packed. As usual, the baggage goes first—then the men.

A day before my evacuation, late Saturday night, I am sitting in my room trying to read by the light of the candle, a Yiddish book. Suddenly my door opens, and a soldier, with his pack still on his shoulders, enters. He greets me quietly, and without asking, sits down opposite me. I regard him for a time. His appearance is terrible. His unruly black beard, his dirty face and torn clothes are not quite to be described, but from his dark face shines forth the most radiant eyes. He remains silent awhile, then blurts out, "Chaplain! You can't imagine what I've been through the last few days." My spontaneous guest stimulates my spirit. I am curious to hear, from beginning to end, what this soldier has to tell me. Indeed, I wish him to describe for me a true picture of the terrible situation at the front.

The dark-faced soldier tells me he has come from a bitter hell. He is a medic. All the wounded in the Seventh Division were brought to his station to receive first aid, such as blood plasma, dressings, injections, etc. Day and night he had been occupied at the front with his nerve-shattering work. One could not find sufficient room for all the wounded, and many remained lying in the snow, in the open air, but these suffered bravely, as true heroes. One heard no complaints from them. They waited patiently until they received help, each in his own turn. Some were totally silent—in their own world. The anguish and pain were severe. One did not eat or drink during these days and nights. A short nap substituted for true sleep.

One night, suddenly, the ugly report came through that the Americans were totally surrounded by the Chinese army. Not far from this position, the Chinese had attacked and shot a unit of sleeping troops. Those who survived the initial onslaught began to run to wherever their eyes led them. The doctors ordered that any wounded that could stand on their feet should save themselves. Some of the wounded crawled on their bellies in deep snow, and when they reached the main road, they first realized that the road had been blocked by the Chinese, who lay in wait for the fleeing casualties.

Meanwhile, from all directions came ambulances and jeeps loaded with troops. The order had been given to break through the blockade. Whoever was fated to live would make it; whoever was not, was doomed. My informant tells me he stayed close to a group of officers, and when the order came to break out, the troop-filled jeeps and trucks began to speed off with great acceleration. Soon, however, they found themselves in a flood of enemy fire. It hailed bullets. There was shooting from every side, and there appeared to be no way out. All saw Death dancing before their eyes. To turn back was impossible. Behind them were masses of refugees. Before them was the enemy fire. Only aboard one of the vehicles was there any chance to avoid certain death. The jeep on which my medic was riding managed to tear through, but two of his companions were killed, and the driver was severely wounded. Alone, he jumped from the jeep into the darkness and hid in a crater beside the road, and then slowly began to crawl on his belly until he had covered enough distance that he no longer heard the crack of the rifles. Tired, exhausted, he wandered, day and night, without eating or sleeping, until he just made it to the American lines.

My narrator speaks of his experiences in great detail, and as he speaks, tears pour from his eyes. "Chaplain," he said, "in the last few days, I have become an old man. I don't think I could come through a horror like this again. This is a terrible war. You don't see the enemy. When you least expect him, he springs out from a dark hiding place and attacks with murder in his heart, with a wild viciousness."

I look at this soldier and think how deep is the disappointment of those who received notice from General MacArthur that they would be going home for the new year, to their loved ones. Instead, they find themselves in the upheaval of a new, hellish battle.

All the great victories of the brave Marines are for naught. All the heroic triumphs were erased at the moment of the new attack by a half-million Chinese soldiers. Our courageous fighters had already been over the border into North Korea. It appeared that the war was nearing its end. Now, how tragic to admit to ourselves that the bold American Marines are surrounded by the enemy, and that they must fight desperately in order to break out of the trap that grows tighter and tighter around them.

Der Morgen Zhornal, January 2, 1951

Moving Scenes as Americans Leave North Korean Harbor

A Visit to a Korean Home

by Chaplain Milton J. Rosen

When the Japanese left Korea after their loss of the Second World War, it was the end of a domination that had lasted forty years. Although they withdrew physically, however, they left behind as an inheritance a great portion of their culture. This influence has been strongly apparent in two generations of the Korean people. The older people in Korea and the very young do not know the Japanese language, but the middle-aged group speaks it fluently and grammatically. It would take six years for a student to learn the language thoroughly. The village people were not affected by the language or the culture, however. Behind the tall, gigantic mountains, Japanese influence did not penetrate. This makes it difficult to communicate with the village population. If one meets a village representative and begins to speak Japanese, he is regarded as a rooster in the society of men.

Currently, one sees only few signs of progress and civilization in Korea. The present war has erased nearly all of it. However, if you should happen upon something beautiful and valuable, you may be sure that it was imported from Japan. Suffice it to say that if you encounter a finely built house, a modern factory, a multistoried building in the midst of the poor, darkened streets, you will be aware that it was built by the Japanese. The majority of the streets and highways in Korea are bad, often badly damaged. The smooth, slippery asphalt roads were paved by the Japanese. The few comfortable transportation vehicles were introduced during Japanese occupation.

The Russians used the modern facilities very well, for their military purposes. In Hungnam, where the headquarters of the American Tenth Corps is now located, whole blocks of large buildings and apartment housing stretch out before the viewer. Especially attractive are the buildings in the area of the harbor. These structures are built of strong brick in Japanese style and possess the most modern facilities. The apartment houses were built by the Japanese especially for workers. The poorer Koreans had not maintained their residences in good condition, and these became neglected and abandoned.

Not far from the tall apartment houses are long blocks of gigantic factories. Now, these buildings are battered and desolate. The bombs that fell on the Japanese during the world war erased the industrial quarter, but the skeletal remains of the factories give testimony to the quality of their previous construction. The Japanese occupiers had sought to curry favor among the downtrodden Koreans by building comfortable, affordable apartment residences close behind the factories.

Life for the Koreans has remained rather primitive, much as it was hundreds of years ago. Perhaps for this reason the average Korean takes such pleasure every time he sees a new American invention. The Korean will tell you, with malevolent delight, that the Russians "possess nothing" to compare with American products. The Korean will grasp in his hands with enormous enthusiasm an American garment or a pair of American shoes, squeeze them on all sides, then express his wonder and pleasure with a whistle. For them, everything is a novelty, a surprise. As one observes this excitement, one is drawn to the conclusion that these people are first emerging from a deep darkness, in which they have been stuck thousands of years. This nation aspires to enlightenment.

It is sad, therefore, to see their reaction, as they observe the Americans leaving their territory, the ships with thousands of Marines and soldiers sailing from their shores. I took a walk and just looked at the faces of the hundreds of Koreans, men, women, and children, who had gathered near the ships, looking on as the American troops were boarding to leave. The Koreans simply wept aloud. They felt destruction approaching. With every mile the Chinese march, the danger grows more ominous. The hatred toward the oncoming enemy and the affection toward the Americans becomes the starker, as even at their departure from this land the American troops are distributing food, shoes, sweaters, socks, and clothing of all sorts to the impoverished population.

A Korean said to me, "the Americans are some peculiar people. The armies of other nations, when they have left the country, have turned the departure date into a day of open robbery. Their soldiers have plundered whatever was left. The looting has always accelerated, and no one has considered the poor defeated people."

As if to confirm the contrast between the others and ourselves, my office was a scene today of such a case in point. Two Jewish soldiers, tired and sweating, came running into my office, and before sitting down, began to recount how they have been going around town collecting food and other goods and distributing them to the people. They intend to do the same tomorrow and the next day. They told me it is the duty of American soldiers to do what they can before they leave. They then asked me if it would be possible to smuggle a few Koreans aboard, to save them from the inevitable destruction and desolation. Of course, I cannot answer such a question, but I was moved by the sincere intentions of our American boys, who never cease to think of these unfortunate people. These young men are the merciful children of merciful people.

The Koreans, themselves, are so filled with terror of that which threatens them that wherever one goes, wherever one stands, people grab hold of one's lapels and ask if they could not be taken along on the journey. They wish to flee wherever opportunity takes them. They want to move speedily to far places. They want to distance themselves from the oncoming enemy, who sows death and destruction.

I do not know how long we will be remaining in North Korea, but I am truly anxious to learn more about Korean life. I run around from one street to the next and hope to be able to enter their houses and stores. The difficulty is that it is not in the nature of the Korean to allow foreigners to get too close. No matter how close, in any case, one is not invited to his home. Despite this, I have simply yearned for an opportunity to be asked, and suddenly, after all, I have succeeded in receiving an invitation. The truth is, I have needed to employ a bit of politics and diplomacy to acquire it.

I had invited a Korean gentleman to my office and received him cordially. He was quite proud to have received the invitation. Think of it! An American officer had received him in his office. My visitor was soon disappointed, however, when I showed him around the other rooms of the post quarters. He saw my bedding on the cold bare floor and realized I possessed no army cot. The place was cold. Outside, the frosty wind raged, and the snow was developing into a blizzard. My guest sat down on a carton and began to lament my difficult fate. He asked about my family in America and about my home. He expressed great sympathy for my loneliness in a strange land, having left my warm, comfortable home, to suffer the cold and dirt of this war. Finally, he told me it would be a great honor if I would visit his house and sleep over for a few nights. His house was humble, but warm. It was heated, incidently, by a stove beneath the floor.

Usually, I do not agree to a house visit. I thanked him for his kindness, but I began to be suspicious; perhaps he is a spy, or maybe he means to rob me. I felt inclined to be rid of him, but he was persistent. He didn't leave. He pressed me with persuasive arguments. I must come. His house is actually not far from the office. Finally, I agreed to accompany him, considering the benefit of this opportunity, at last, to view a simple Korean home.

His house is located in a narrow, muddy street. In front is a glass door. From the outside, it looks like a shop. In the first room are stacked used tin cans, a bicycle, a refrigerator and various pieces of scrap iron, as if it were a junk dealership. Soon, another door opens before me, Japanese in style, and we remove our shoes before crossing the threshold. The floor is very dirty, but my host spreads clean straw mats, and I stroll about in my stockinged feet. He offers me an old chair. We smoke cigarettes and begin to talk. Almost at once, from a side door, appears a naked child, about two years of age, so dirty and unkempt, one could hardly describe it. His wife appears, but he does not introduce her. Apparently, that is their custom. I look around. A door opens from the right. A second door opens from the left, and now, for the first time, I have a picture, close up, of the intimate life of a Korean family. But more of this later.

Der Morgen Zhornal, January 7, 1951

The Trap That the Chinese Had Prepared for the Americans in Korea

by Chaplain Milton J. Rosen

For the American troops surrounded in North Korea, there were two choices: either break through the fiery blockade or allow themselves to be taken captive. The General had ordered, "better to die than to give ourselves up to the enemy," and the disciplined, courageous Marines obeyed the General. They jumped into the flames of battle like flies, and, unfortunately, they also fell like flies. Their determination to fight to the last man, rather than surrender, pushed them to offer a heroic, but desperate resistance. Across the battlefield, seemingly without end, lay the wounded. It was impossible to reach them on foot to administer first-aid. The only way to reach them was by air, and indeed, squadrons of aircraft were sent to bring them out to the hospital stations.

It is difficult enough for those near to the place of the tragedy, and certainly more difficult for those more distant, to paint for themselves the horrid, hellish scenes that play themselves out on the battlefield. What extraordinary emotion overcomes you when you see hundreds of trucks packed with wounded Marines, still wearing their camouflage gear, covered with dust, exhausted, frozen, dirty, slowly moving along the long way back. Most of the wounded wear only their bloody uniforms. The more fortunate possess a blanket, which warms the shoulders and back. These American Marines pass before me in retreat, but they remain the undaunted heroes who have fought for the defense of human freedom.

The worst manifestations of the battlefield are the inevitable chaos, the unexpected panic, the forced retreat. One never knows if today's daily routine will be the same tomorrow. One receives a telephone order, for example, to report to officer X tomorrow at office Y. When he arrives at the appointed hour there is no one to be found. The clerks will have removed the tables, the chairs, the stacks of papers—all taken to another place. A joke circulates around Korea that one can invite another for dinner, set the table, light the lamps, but when the guest arrives, the host is no longer to be found.

A refreshing break in the depressed atmosphere occurs at the sight of the open sea. The numerous ships anchored in the harbor offer encouragement. The ships symbolize the bridge to the free world. If we need to withdraw, we know the comfort of the proximity of this fleet. It is, in our minds, a direct connection to America and home.

Day and night, the planes fly overhead, not individually, but in virtual caravans, on their way to the battlefield. On a good day, when the sky is clear and bright, we know true joy. The American Air Force provides the protection that will help save the encircled troops.

It is a frosty early morning. I decide to go out to the town market to purchase a few necessaries. This is quite a market. The whole area is about 100 × 150 feet. Here, there are wooden carts packed with all sorts of food articles and other merchandise. Usually there is also a bit of black market activity, as well. On a pretty day, the press of the crowd is so intense one can hardly navigate among the multitudes.

I go into a small store that sells needles and thread. I greet the storekeeper in Japanese. The proprietor is most surprised to hear me speak Japanese and becomes quite friendly. I look behind me and note that I am surrounded by a cluster of people. Most of them are young students, who hang around aimlessly. They speak to me of many things, but the main subject is the Chinese invasion. One of the students admits the Koreans made a great error when they overlooked the Chinese threat. They simply never thought of the possibility of a Chinese attack. He is convinced the current situation will be worse than under the Japanese. The Koreans are poor enough, he muses, but the Chinese will make them poorer.

Another student tells me of the Russian military, which had previously been stationed here in great numbers. The Russians, he said, would simply plunder the markets. They robbed the poor merchants. They would grab girls off the street and take them where they would. That time was truly disastrous.

Why must the Americans leave? Wherever the Americans have gone, they have brought revived hope. Now, there hovers a sense of hopelessness and panic. What is there left for these helpless people to do in view of the Chinese danger?

I can offer no comfort to the desperate Koreans. I tell them the essential element for a people is unity. They must hold together and support the ideals of the United Nations. Suddenly, one of the students jumps up and cries out that Communism will ruin Korea forever, and only the United Nations can restore the land to its previous independence and security. I hear in the comments of the students a regret for the neglect of many national problems.

As of this moment, I have found no Jews in Korea. No matter how many people I have asked regarding Jewish inhabitants, I have received no adequate reply. I am also unable to ascertain whether there had been a Jewish population earlier on. The question torments me, and I have made myself a promise that wherever I go in Korea, I will seek intensely my fellow Jews.

I have noted a peculiar characteristic of the Koreans, that as soon as they meet you they want to know your age. If you tell them, for example, that you are forty-one years old, they will emit a groan and tell you that you look much older. They also have a tendency to ask you to guess their age. They laugh gleefully when you err in this estimate. The foreign visitor will guess the Korean to be younger than he or she actually is, for the Koreans keep themselves young, in spite of the heavy burdens they carry year after year on their backs. They are used to their poverty. They regard suffering as a natural occurrence, against which one cannot fight, and one does not bother himself over the details of daily living. Indeed, they have scant concern over that which will occur tomorrow. It seems this very freedom from worry and fear maintains their youthfulness. Many manners and customs among the Koreans are strikingly different from ours. What appears to the American to be shameful is regarded as natural among the Koreans. A Korean woman, for example, will nurse her child freely on the street, lifting the upper part of her garment without inhibition. This appears to be very common among the Korean women, and no one regards it as less than moral or inconsistent with modesty.

I managed a bit of conversation with a Korean who had asked me for some medicine for his cold. We spoke of various illnesses, and I eventually asked him if there is much venereal disease in Korea. The Korean answered with pride that in Korea there never was such a sickness and never will be, because the Koreans are a highly moral people, which does not promote intimate relations between men and women. He did not fail to add that in Japan and America, the illness was indeed widespread. In Korea, he continued, men are true to their wives and maintain family purity.

Strange that one sees no newspapers at all. At several places in town, however, placards with large script are posted daily, giving the latest news. The news is brief and precise and is an exact reproduction of that which one hears over the radio. The armed forces mix very little with the population, and often the civilian knows much earlier what is happening at the front than does the soldier. The Koreans even know which cities have been captured by the Chinese at a time when the Americans have not learned of it.

Meanwhile, the roads are jammed with refugees, seeking sanctuary in the mountains before the Chinese enemy arrives. These are the foresighted ones, the nimble ones, who take their bag and baggage and embark on their way, in anticipation of the new disaster. The general consensus is that the Chinese are coming to take over that which the Japanese had had to give up.

War or no war, my work as Jewish chaplain must go on. To my hut, which we may be using only a few more days, come, as usual, Jewish soldiers from the surrounding areas with their rifles over their shoulders. They are coming for spiritual solace. They come on Friday night to celebrate the gift of the Sabbath. We chant together the Kiddush, the prayer that sanctifies the Sabbath, the day of rest, while war planes zoom overhead. We sing "peace be with you," but there is no peace.

Der Morgen Zhornal, January 9, 1951

Koreans Regret That Jews Never Settled in Their Country

Pictures of the Intimate Life of a Korean Household

by Chaplain Milton J. Rosen

Sitting as a guest in the modest house of a Korean family, speaking comfortably with the head of the household about the situation at the war fronts, I noticed through the door opposite me a second room, in which a young woman about thirty was sitting. She sat quite relaxed, before a walled mirror, combing her long hair. She glanced at me and offered a smile of greeting.

At first I paid no special attention to her, but after a time I was drawn to the scene that was unfolding before my eyes. As she continued quietly, languidly combing her hair, she started literally popping lice with her free hand, as they fell from the comb. Every time she pulled the comb through her hair, she would kill lice, with apparent pleasure and without embarrassment. She was not in the least reticent. My presence as an American officer and an invited guest did not concern her. She performed her task as naturally as an American woman would powder her face. Her husband looked on and smiled. I had the impression he was very proud of his wife, who was demonstrating her fastidiousness for his company.

Be that as it may, I declined his offer to spend the night in his warm house.

It is night. I am sitting in my cold room, writing a letter by the dim light of a tallow candle. There is a blackout, which has been ordered because of an expected enemy air raid. The goal of the Chinese is the destruction of our airfield and planes.

The blackout lasts a long time, and even when it is over, the electric lights are not restored to my room, so I continue writing by the glow of the candle. Abruptly, the door opens and a Korean enters, introducing himself as Dr. Hing Bang Hok.

He tells me he has wanted to meet me for a long time. I offer him a chair. He sits and begins to speak to me in fluent English. I learn that he completed his medical studies at the University of Seoul, Korea. Later on, he traveled to America to take a post-graduate course at Severence Medical College in Virginia. He is in line for the top job at the Health Department in Korea and is a member of the Tenth Corps for Civilian Affairs.

What he wants from me is my precise opinion regarding the situation here. He, himself, is a native of Hungnam and knows the people of this region very well. He is aware of the terror that has gripped the population, and he, himself, has not been able to sleep through a full night because of the thousands of people who live in panic. They are convinced that if the Chinese push into the city, the North Korean Communists will take the opportunity to revenge themselves for their earlier defeat and will kill many decent, innocent citizens of the area.

The desperate doctor asked me what, as a medical man, he can do for these frightened Koreans. We plan. We seek solutions. Perhaps it would be practical to acquire several ships to carry these unfortunate people to more secure places? The doctor tells me he has no rest. He runs around day and night seeking means and ways to save these people. He knows, in fact, that several ships are indeed prepared to transport a few thousand.

Looking at the doctor, I get an impression of the mood of the Korean people. I hear in his words an echo of the lament and grief of those who long to leave here as soon as possible.

The doctor is a young man, about twenty-eight years of age, but he looks much older. Wrinkles and creases of profound old age have been engraved upon his face. He carries on his shoulders the heavy burden of the anguish with which his people live.

As we continue talking intimately of the serious situation in Korea, I am suddenly moved to ask my visitor whether he could give me any information about the Jewish people and Korea. He informs me that actually there have never been Jews living in Korea. The only knowledge Koreans have about Jews is that which they have learned from Christian missionaries in their religious schools. The doctor is aware of the fact that during World War II, the Japanese, under the pressure of the Germans, attempted to instill a hatred of the Jewish people, but since the Koreans had never actually seen any Jews, the propaganda, as a matter of course, had no effect on them. Incidentally, to this information he adds his regret that Jews never settled in Korea. Odd, I think. There are countries where we do live, where, in the eyes of the anti-Semite, there are too many of us, and, on the other hand, where we have not lived, they yearn for us.

Of course, the Korean physician has his own motives for desiring Jewish settlements in his country. If Jews, he contends, had settled earlier in Korea, perhaps the land would not have suffered such poverty and backwardness. He counts off the names of great Jewish scientists. He tells me of a well-known professor, a fine physician, Dr. Cooper, who was his teacher. If only Jews had inhabited the land, he thinks, it would have been a source of blessing and good fortune. In Harbin, states my visitor, there were indeed Jews in great numbers and some even became wealthy, but they never came to Korea.

After an evening of unloading his heartfelt concerns, the doctor arises, says goodnight, and goes away, intent on seeking further ways and means to save more people before the advent of the fearful enemy.

I leave my office and go up to my cold room. I prepare myself to lie down on my bedding, which is spread out on the hard, stone floor. Before I go to sleep, however, I must light a candle and place it at the head of my bedding. If I fail to do this, mice and rats will be my guests. What I describe here is by no means exaggeration. Large rats visit me regularly every night. A couple of nights ago, during a sweet sleep, I began to dream that a rat came up to me and began to chew my head with great appetite. I woke up and determined that this was no dream. In actuality, a very real rat stood over me and chewed my hair with delight.

Since that time, I light a candle nightly before retiring. The problem is that the rats are undaunted by the candles. They are insolent and show no manners to anyone, even the chaplain. One can holler, rap, or throw chairs, but they have no fear. Unperturbed, they eat the paper off the walls. After all, they are the early settlers in these houses, and I am the sojourner, the stranger, disturbing their rest.

Lying on my bedding, I look about at the windows and the doors, which have been framed in Japanese style. I see that the paper has been torn and bitten by the rats. I apply all the terror methods I know to drive them away, but it does not help. Even when I throw a heavy boot at them, trying to kill at least one, the gang members move not at all, as if I did not mean it for them. My only protection is the candle. The flame does seem to keep them from coming too close.

"This is some country," I thought. "Even the rats are stubborn, like the North Korean Communists. You drive them back, but they return, currently with their new compatriots, the Chinese Communists."

Der Morgen Zhornal, January 14, 1951

An Unusual Friday Night with Jewish American Soldiers in Korea

Panic in the Civilian Population in Korea

by Chaplain Milton J. Rosen

The most powerful fantasy cannot describe that which a person experiences in the terrible moments of war. It has been my destiny to be a Jewish chaplain in such a place where it is my lot to witness the whole horror of battles, panic, and endless terror.

When, on the first of December, I arrived at my headquarters in Hamhung, I had barely stepped over the threshold of my office when the Colonel chaplain greeted me. There, before I had time to recover from the difficult ship's passage and the long train ride, I was given to understand that it was not worthwhile to unpack. Rather, it was better to prepare to leave this place, for such a command could come any minute. I did not require a great deal of persuasion to look about and recognize that this is a dangerous area. I have already written, in a previous description, about the hundreds of wounded soldiers who passed by me on the way to the hospital. The situation was becoming more hazardous hour by hour. We knew the enemy was pulling ever closer. All the planning for our evacuation was complete. Every section of this large army was quietly to bundle off to Hungnam, which is only several miles from the harbor. There lay all sorts of ships for the rescue of the thousands of soldiers and the badly wounded from impending destruction.

The impatience to leave this place had been growing. Every one of us wanted sooner, rather than later, to get out of this threatened area, where a contest of strength with the enemy is useless. I peered out of the window of my office and remarked on the endless lines of trucks, packed with troops, moving by. I observed the rows of tanks and wagons full of every kind of military equipment. All were pulling out of the city. The larger retreat began at 6:00 p.m. when the curfew went into effect and all the inhabitants had to draw back into their homes, behind locked doors. Our withdrawal had the appearance of a silent, stealthy flight.

The windowpanes rattled from the noise of the heavy war machines as they moved by. From the mountains came also the echo of heavy artillery fire. This was our artillery. It informed the enemy we are still here in strength. It also made it possible to hold the enemy at a respectable distance, to give our troops more time to evacuate. It was very late that night when I finally fell asleep on my hard bed. In the morning, the whole city was covered with snow, although the sky was clear, and the sun shown through in a most friendly manner. The clear sky is a great comfort to us, for in this weather our planes fly into the battle zone and drop their deadly loads upon the enemy. Every bombardment weakens the Chinese and strengthens us.

Finally, the order arrived to leave the area. There ensued a stampede, a rush in every corner of our headquarters. We packed and loaded everything we could, and then we waited impatiently for the trucks that would take us from here. Finally, on the trucks, we all wore steel helmets. The guards held loaded rifles and placed themselves in strategic parts of the trucks. In the streets, the traffic was heavy and noisy. Trucks and jeeps joined from every direction. Also, civilians, with their poor belongings, filled up wagons. They have no specific plan as to where they should run, but they flee desperately, wherever their eyes take them. The congestion, therefore, became greater, more fearful.

When we finally arrived in Hungnam we were settled in the finer houses, left behind by the Japanese, of which I wrote earlier. After several days I was properly arranged in my new quarters.

The first Friday night religious services were held in my house. Jewish soldiers from Brooklyn, from Philadelphia, came to services, their rifles slung over their shoulders. We sang the Sabbath song "Shalom Aleichem," peace be with you, hoping every minute that no bombardment would suddenly interrupt. After the usual prayers were said, we chanted the Kiddush, the sanctification of the Sabbath, and drank the sacramental wine. We ate gefilte fish and matzos. The exhausted Jewish soldiers were thrilled with this traditional Sabbath meal, and they thanked God for the Jewish Welfare Board, the Jewish institution that is so dedicated to the welfare of the Jewish soldiers and which did not forsake them, even in distant Hungnam. Some of the soldiers, among them Harry Cohen from Pittsburgh, Jerry Finkelstein from Newark, New Jersey, and Abe Silverman from Brooklyn, asked me to mention them through *Der Morgen Zhornal,* the respected Jewish newspaper. Their family and their relations read the paper regularly, and this would be an opportunity to greet their loved ones directly from the front.

Our resting period did not last long. After a few days rumors circulated that we shall have to evacuate our current position as well. Already, the artillery fire is now directed toward us. Suddenly the cannon reports are so strong that windowpanes fall out.

On one occasion I went into the mess hall to drink a cup of coffee. My eyes came to rest on the mighty mountains around us, which are covered in orderly fashion by the enemy's tanks. Between each tank is a calculated distance. The enemy tanks fire, but the powerful cannon roar comes from our warships. The exchange of fire between our ships and their tanks is a drawn out battle and a grim contest of power.

At night the panic grows stronger. The artillery fire is heavier. Every hour the guards run around shouting, "turn out the lights! turn on the lights!" In this fashion we get through the sleepless night. This goes on for days, and in the bright skies whole armadas of aircraft fly over in an endless stream, like flocks of birds. "Where do we go from here?" thinks every individual in his heart. The uncertainty destroys the nerves. Impatience tears a man apart. We fear we may pass up the opportunity to get out in time, and as we look out the window and see others on their way to the harbor, we are most envious. The jealousy at that moment is not to be described.

As the artillery fire increases in intensity, so increases the gloom of the Korean population. It is the gloom of deep resignation. The Korean workers, men and women who work at headquarters, go on doing their daily duties as if nothing were happening. The carpenters are finishing up several new doors and windows in a house opposite us, where the officers billeted there are preparing to leave.

Everything that is done here now is camouflage. We continue to build in order not to exhibit to the Koreans our intent to pull out of here. The new accommodations are provisional. As soon as the last soldier leaves the territory, everything will be burned.

A couple of hours after receiving the report that we would leave this place at night, I go once again into the mess hall to drink a cup of coffee. Here, everything is quiet, as if nothing were occurring. The Koreans who serve the food give no indication of nervousness. Those who are eating digest their food as they did before. My heart tells me that the order for us to leave tonight is no more than a drill, an exercise to prepare for later.

As it turns out, I have not fooled myself. We were not evacuated during

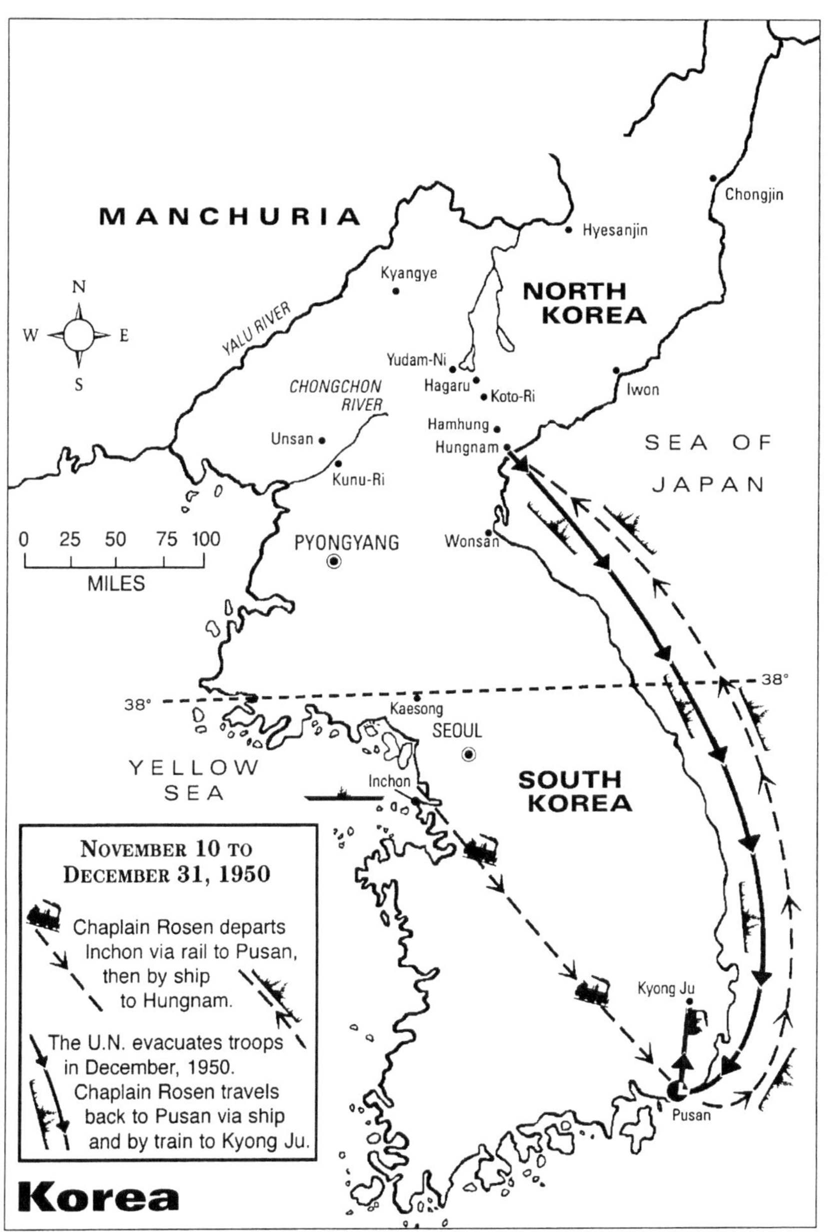

Schematic of Chaplain Rosen's transport to and from the Battlefield, November 10 to December 31, 1950.

this night. Our army apparently must see the eyes of the Chinese up close in order to leave the territory.

The night has been full of nightmares. No one has slept. The artillery cracked without surcease. The noise of the shooting could drive one mad. At times, it seemed the walls might collapse. The windows are broken, the lights are out, and the floor has been shaking as if per an earthquake.

It is now the day following. It is Friday. The cannonade has apparently stopped. All morning, from early on, I have been receiving visitors, frightened Korean inhabitants who beg me with tears in their eyes to take them with me onto the ship. Some of them are certain that the Communists will kill them as soon as the Americans leave. They cry aloud. The weeping soon acquires a community quality, as others keep coming in through various doors, and the room soon takes on the atmosphere of a solemn dirge. As comfort, all I can do is distribute packets of cigarettes and chocolate. They take their leave sadly, but with expressions of hope that we may meet again in happier times.

The day begins to sink. In the air one begins to feel the arrival of the Sabbath, the transition from the mundane to the holy. As the time for the Friday night prayers nears, about 7:00 p.m., Jewish soldiers come to me from all directions. Those who had shared the Friday night Sabbath celebration eight days ago are not here. Perhaps they are already aboard ship. I see new faces, who come seeking comfort and encouragement. In my house only candles are burning. The electric lights are out.

It is an unusual Friday night. It is dim in the house, but our mood is bright. We sing the greeting to the Sabbath with warm enthusiasm. We recite, "Cause us to lie down in peace," most sincerely. We say with great conviction, "turn away from us enemy, pestilence, and sword." Oh how these words seem so significant at this moment. The words are, however, interrupted by the thunder of artillery. When the prayers have come to an end, the soldiers eat their gefilte fish from the can. They are pleasantly surprised when I honor them with kosher salami, a treat that is eaten with great delight. It brings to mind the pleasures of our far away homes. My parents would never have believed that here, under the din of artillery shells, thousands of miles from home, literally under the wings of death, I sit in a dark house on Friday night and eat freshly opened salami and matzos.

Chaplain Milton J. Rosen, Japan, 1948. Courtesy Stanley R. Rosen.

Chaplain Rosen alighting from transport, on one of his trips to military units in Japan, circa 1948. Courtesy Stanley R. Rosen.

Chaplain Rosen with member of Tokyo Jewish Community before Jewish Chapel Center, 1949. Courtesy Stanley R. Rosen.

Chaplain Rosen officiating at bar mitzvah ceremony of young member of Tokyo Jewish Community. Father (assumed) of bar mitzvah at left. Courtesy Stanley R. Rosen.

Chaplain Rosen blowing traditional ram's horn, marking the High Holy Days, at the Jewish Chapel Center, Yokohama Command. Photograph by U.S. Army photographer Prouty.

Bon voyage to Chaplain Rosen, from many Japanese friends, returning to the United States from first tour of duty, summer of 1950. Courtesy Stanley R. Rosen.

Editor Stanley Rosen (*second from left*) on Passover leave, with his father, Chaplain Rosen, at Seder in Japan, 1954. Courtesy Stanley R. Rosen.

7
Pusan Again

Back in southeastern Korea, Chaplain Rosen docked, at first, in Pusan, only to be sent north by rail to the mountainous area of Kyongju. However, it was not too long before he was returned to Pusan, to headquarter there, using it as a base for excursions to various units in the greater surrounding area, seeking Jewish soldiers, offering his services as chaplain. The chilling memory of all they had been through was still fresh in the minds of the soldiers and Marines as the New Year began, and the articles written at this time reflect this. General Walker had been killed in a traffic accident and had been replaced by Lieutenant General Matthew Ridgeway, who took command of a rather disconsolate army, a condition he was determined to alter. He had at his disposal over 350,000 men, in three U.S. Corps, I, IX, and X, two ROK Corps, small Turkish and Commonwealth units, and support units. Against this were about four to five hundred thousand Chinese and North Korean battle-hardened troops, not considering their reserves of manpower. It became apparent over time, however, that the expenditure of men and materiel in intense battles would be felt by the Communist forces to perhaps a greater degree than had at first been appreciated, leaving them temporarily rather exhausted at intervals. General Ridgeway determined to use this revelation to good advantage, directing his forces and the might of his armor and air superiority to inflict enormous casualties on the enemy, for one thing, and cautiously advancing to more beneficial positions, when the enemy was depleted, for another. Thus, although in January the enemy had made solid inroads into the line of the U.N. troops, including possession of Seoul, by mid-January,

General Ridgeway began to move up stage by stage, as the force of the Communist offensive waned, to halfway between the farthest enemy penetration and Seoul in the west and a comparable line in the east. A second drive inaugurated not only greater resistance but also a counterattack east of Seoul, at Chipyong-ni, which was eventually blunted, the latter event opening the way for Operation Killer, directed at destroying Communist forces in the eastern portion of the front. This was followed by other initiatives, until at the end of March the U.N. armies were, essentially, back at the 38th parallel. Ultimately, the U.N. troops under Ridgeway were well enough positioned at and above the 38th parallel to effect sufficient attrition of Communist troops that overtures for negotiation could be realistically considered. General MacArthur's independent and contrary positions to those of President Truman soon led to the former's dismissal. This led to Ridgeway's elevation to Chief of the Far East Command and to the appointment of General James Van Fleet as Field Commander in place of General Ridgeway. General Van Fleet maintained much the same military posture as that of General Ridgeway, with the approval of the administration, and was in charge during the long and wearying two years of negotiations that followed.

8

Der Morgen Zhornal Articles January 16, 1951–March 11, 1951

Der Morgen Zhornal, January 16, 1951

When the American Soldiers Left the North Korean Harbor City

Jewish Soldiers Receive the Order Friday Night, at Prayer, to Leave the City

by Chaplain Milton J. Rosen

As I was sitting with the Jewish soldiers on Friday night, by the dim light of nearly exhausted candles, a sudden chill blew in through the broken window.

We had been speaking with longing of returning to the United States, as if describing a distant dream, and if not to America, then at least to Japan. These soldiers went on to confide various episodes of their battlefield experiences. The longer, extended discussion centered on the latest developments in the war. In the midst of the conversation, my division chaplain appeared and told us quickly to clear out to the road, as in about a half an hour we would be leaving this place. This meant that the Jewish soldiers had to return hastily to their quarters.

In fact, exactly thirty minutes later, I was completely ready and on my way, steel helmet on my head, food packs on my shoulders, and my blanket bound up in a sack. The rest of the baggage was quickly loaded onto the truck that awaited us. Together with several other chaplains from our corps, I climbed onto the truck, and before we could even look around, the heavy wheels had begun rolling over the streets.

The city was dead still. The darkness was dense, uncanny. From time to time, we heard the thunder of artillery. No other trucks or jeeps accompanied us. We stole out individually so that no one would know we were evacuating.

The night was calm and beautiful, but unusually cold. The snow that had fallen earlier had already been melted by the day's sun. None of the passengers spoke a word. The truck rode easily, without haste, until we arrived at the harbor.

As deadly quiet as the city had been, so, in contrast, was the racket in the harbor. Hundreds of soldiers, with their bag and baggage, awaited their ships. Countless trucks, jeeps, tanks, and wagons, with various materials, stood here in long lines. The ships grasped the heavy loads and swallowed them into their interiors. The noise and din deafened the ears. The cold became ever more intense, and fires burned in every corner, lit by the soldiers to keep themselves a little warmer. Among the mass of soldiers, one could see many South Koreans. I noted even the Korean girls who worked as servers in the mess halls and in the kitchens. They too were shivering with cold and wished as quickly as possible to be rescued from this place, hopefully with the first ship. Their lives were in danger if the enemy should appear. Any Korean who demonstrated loyalty to the Americans was automatically sentenced to death by the Communists. Certainly these Koreans, even the young kids who served as "houseboys," were taken aboard ship. The children were dressed as the soldiers were. The Americans dressed them and treated them as they would their own children. The boarding of the hundreds of soldiers took many hours. Aboard ship, the troubles first really began. It became clear that the ship was not built for passengers or supplies. There was no place to sleep. The number of troops was very large. The cramping grew ever worse. Necessity forced each one to look after himself. The ship had five separate, large rooms. The officers climbed down iron ladders and disappeared into the depths of the ship. The soldiers found place in the great rooms and in the corridors. One twisted and shoved and compressed. I lay my bedding upon the cold, stony floor. My territory was no more than five cubits. In the narrow space, we simply crawled over each other.

Because we were all so tired, we fell asleep almost immediately. The hard bed was no obstacle. How sweet is the sleep of the tired out soldier. The cold, the noise, the exhaustion brought to all a pleasant deep sleep.

The night was a short one. In the morning, I learned that the loading of the heavy cargo had dragged on the whole night, and only around 8:00 a.m. did the ship actually begin to cut the waters. Where we were going, no one knew. One tried to guess. Perhaps to Pusan? If not there, where? It would mean that we were coming back to the very place we started to fight, a month ago.

One cannot hide the fact that it was a troubled voyage. Forget about the hard bed. The cold, one can withstand. However, there were not even the basic facilities a person requires. There were already many voices criticizing the arrangements. The American army, said the dissatisfied, spends a great deal of money on unnecessary and useless things, but doesn't concern itself regarding the most elemental necessities. It was indeed awful to observe people forced to live in filth and in truly unacceptable conditions.

As support for the complaints of the critics, the fact may be brought forth that during the ten days we were in Hungnam the carpenters were very busy making new windows and doors, which would later be burned down, but no orders were given to construct toilet facilities or a bath or shower for bodily hygiene. Needless to say, small things had their effect on the morale of the troops. The conclusion may be drawn that a person in the Army has no intrinsic value. His presence is of no significance—and this occurs in the army of the richest land in the world.

The soldiers spoke with great bitterness about what they saw in Inchon. They complained that the Army had spent too much money on building an officers' club with a bar, but they forgot to build a washroom and an adequate facility for necessities of life.

No less a complaint was heard regarding the food distribution on the ship. The soldiers, who stood in long lines with their metal mess kits and cutlery, were dissatisfied with the cold, canned food they were dispensed three times a day. The same meal for breakfast, lunch, and supper tends to be eaten quickly. Therefore, they would pop into the kitchen from time to time to see if they could get a hot coffee or a sandwich. Because of the cramped conditions below, many soldiers slept on deck. The cold on deck of the ship is unceasing, and it is understandable that after such a night's sleep, under the open skies, it would be easy to acquire a cold.

I was sitting in the small dining area where the ship's crew would eat, when

I heard a young lieutenant complain he had no warm clothes. The story went that the night we left Hungnam the warehouses were emptied. The merchandise was loaded onto trucks or transport to be burned. The trucks contained new, heavy, warm overcoats. The soldiers who suspected that the trucks had clothing aboard took two and three overcoats apiece. Then, those who came later seeking overcoats were told that all had been handed out.

The voyage lasted two days and two nights before we finally arrived at Pusan. It would have been good, after a tiring trip such as that which we had just passed, if we could have caught our breath and washed up a bit. However, with hardly enough time to dust off our feet, we received the news that immediately after leaving the ship, we would travel another seventy miles, into a deep wasteland.

Der Morgen Zhornal, January 18, 1951

The Tragedy of the Korean Civilians Fleeing Their Communist Attackers

Scenes and Pictures from behind the Battle Lines

by Chaplain Milton J. Rosen

It was during the time following the evacuation when our army took up its temporary stations in camps throughout the Korean war zone. On a cold, snowy day, a Catholic chaplain came into camp accompanied by a small, Korean boy. The chaplain was one of the very last to leave Hungnam. His arrival seemed to stimulate little interest among the soldiers, but this was certainly not true of his young companion, who followed him like a helpless babe after its mother.

The boy was dressed in Army clothing. His overcoat hung about his body. Into his trousers, one could easily have stuck another child of similar height and weight. He was a poignant little boy with dark, glowing eyes. No one knew how and from where he arrived in this situation. Curiosity led to questions, and before long there emerged a tragic story of a shattered family, one of those genuine, unembellished incidents of life created by this bloody war.

In brief, as the harbor at Hungnam was being gradually encircled by the enemy, when the coast and the sea were the only source of escape, thousands upon thousands of Korean refugees were fleeing their homes. They grabbed only those belongings they could carry on their backs and their heads. They gathered in a designated area with the single hope that the Korean government or the United Nations would provide them with ships on which they could escape to Pusan. The panic engendered by the desperate effort to save themselves led to terrible confusion in which whole families were torn apart, men separated from their wives, children lost from their parents. The youngster of whom I speak had been with his mother and two sisters at the time the American convoys began moving out to Hungnam Harbor. The terrified masses began running in all directions, to join the convoys. The mother was forced to be separated from the boy "only for a while"—and so she believed it to be. The convoy, however, was extremely long. The troops kept coming, endlessly. Hundreds and thousands of people were transported by various routes, and in this process, the child was lost.

He wandered about over roads and fields until he was seen by an M.P., who took the boy aboard his jeep, and, seeking a guardian for the homeless youngster, he thought to bring him to the Catholic chaplain. The latter did, indeed, pity the unfortunate child, dressed him in a uniform and took him along aboard the ship. Now he has turned up in this camp. What will be done now, however, with the young refugee, no one seems to know. It is not just the problem of this stray boy, but also the problem of the refugees in all of Korea, for which no one has a solution. Aside from this youngster, there are around Pusan perhaps seventy thousand refugees. Actually, he might well utter a prayer. Perhaps his parents have been saved from war's hell fire and may even now be found among those being held on the neighboring island.

Many stray refugees are being consistently brought to this small island not far from Pusan. On the last transport were seventy thousand newly arrived people from the villages around Hamhung and Hungnam, the cities that have been essentially emptied of inhabitants. Aboard every small S.T. boat, some eight hundred soldiers can be evacuated, as they are rescued from the Chinese entrapment. In truth, however, currently, there are generally around fifteen hundred souls, with the addition of the refugees. One can imagine the cramping and the suffocating closeness of the desperate passengers. One takes these troubles in stride, however, for everyone knows these problems are temporary. The desire is to get away from this hellish war zone as soon as possible. However, one does not know what tomorrow will bring. Perhaps, heaven forbid, the United Nations could decide that the armies should leave Korea entirely. Then, where would the poor refugees go? Who would help them in their predicament? The victorious North Koreans and the Chinese Communists sharpen their knives for revenge on the civilian population, which was friendly to the Americans—and there lies the great tragedy.

A chaplain who had been active in Korea for twenty-five years as a missionary, and who has a fluent command of the Korean language, had just arrived in our camp from Pusan. He told us terrible details regarding the wanderings of the fleeing people and the disintegration of families. The tragedy in Korea, he held, is the greatest illustration of the tendency of the world to bring itself to destruction. It requires great strength and resistance to avoid a catastrophe.

I had learned a few days earlier that there is a bathhouse in town. A bath.

I must confess that since I have been in Korea I have not once had the pleasure of a real bath. Only in such cities as Pusan and Seoul can a military man have such a privilege. In the distant, far-flung towns, one must often forego even the most elementary principals of hygiene.

No sooner had the news regarding the city bath become known to us, than the soldiers began streaming in. I also had an overwhelming longing to take a hot bath. I did ask about the status of hygiene in the facilities and received sufficient satisfaction to warrant my trip to the baths.

The small house that offers the baths is a miniature structure in the Japanese style. There are two compartments, one for men and one for women. As soon as one enters, one encounters a venerable old man with a small pointed beard. He sits between the two sections in position to see what is happening on either side of the dividing curtain. Both men and women must pay him for the privilege of entering the bath. The entry tickets cost a total of one hundred won each, which, in American currency, amounts to about two and one-half cents. The old man does his job with an air of indifference.

He sits on his bench with a sort of stoic calm, concerning himself very little with his status as a male, as he daily oversees Eve's daughters, as well as Adam's sons, going about as did, at one time, Adam and Eve in the Garden of Eden, before eating of the tree of knowledge.

The custom here is to remove one's shoes at the very entrance. Everyone receives a box into which to place his things. When completely undressed, one enters another small room, which is well heated. Here, there are small wooden buckets. The bather takes a bucket and draws water from a pool. He soaps himself well and then dips in the pool. The water level in the pools is very low and one must kneel if the water is to cover above the knees.

In spite of small inconveniences, here and there, the bath is a truly refreshing experience for every soldier. It is such a pleasure to wash thoroughly after such long wandering. From the other side of the wall can be heard the sighs of the old ladies and the sounds of the young women with their children. It seems that the excursion to the bathhouse is a very attractive pastime for the Koreans, a festive experience, not just when entering. Also, as they leave, they carry their towels and baskets with the pride of marchers in a parade.

My curiosity impelled me to take a walk through the city. I walked through the streets dotted with poor shops and noted that nearly all the merchandise on the shelves was purchased from American soldiers. The articles consisted of all sorts of candy, cigarettes, chewing gum, and similar objects. The expense is considerable. Generally, the merchants hold the merchandise for the civilian Koreans, rather than for the Americans. The American can purchase other merchandise without paying a penny in cash. He needs only to have with him his cigarettes, chewing gum, and candy. If you would wish to buy back that pack of chewing gum that the Korean had purchased from the American soldier, you would have to pay a fortune, because the merchants are inclined to charge exorbitant prices.

Today I had my big boots polished, as they were very muddy. The shoe polisher, a young man, asked me for six hundred won, which translated to fifteen cents. I asked him whether a package of candy "Charms" would satisfy him. The boy smiled and exclaimed, "okay!" He will be able to sell the candy for a thousand won. In America, the pack costs only a nickel, and I acquired it on my ration card for nothing. So he and I conducted business, making for a lively world. So it is with business in Korea. It is in any case better than Russian borsht or Chinese cuisine.

Incidentally, it is worth mentioning that there is a strong inflation in South Korea. Everything is very expensive because the Americans had been here over an extensive period and spent a lot of money. In North Korea, the won stands higher. I have observed that in North Korea, both currencies are in circulation whether at the Communist value standard or that of South Korea. On the other hand, in South Korea, the people recognize only their own money. A citizen of South Korea will hand back in anger a money bill from North Korea, if you should attempt to purchase merchandise with it.

Der Morgen Zhornal, January 23, 1951

How the Chinese Spies Seek Information in the American Army in Korea

The Retreat at the River Yalu

by Chaplain Milton J. Rosen

It is now several days in which we find ourselves in an indeterminate status. The situation is neither here nor there. No one knows where in the world we stand. What are the latest plans? What is the next strategic move? Are we preparing to leave Korea, or will we soon mount a strong offensive to destroy the enemy?

Today this is the most likely subject of conversation, whether at headquarters or in the camps, which spread deeply through the valley that lies at the foot of the mountains of Kyongju. We have no radio. We get no press releases. The only newspaper we see is the *Stars and Stripes,* a dry Army paper, lacking pepper and salt. The majority of our news is reprinted from old newspapers, or we are fed short, aging reports, gathered from radio news.

So we live in shadow and darkness, unable to discern what is current and reliable. For this reason, one hears many rumors, but the latter are full of contradictions. One piece of news is the exact opposite of the next piece of news. We acquired one report that as of the end of January (this month), there will not remain one single American soldier in Korea. There is considerable betting going on, even beyond money. People are putting up shoes, shirts, overcoats. The noise of the wagering is as loud as if we were at a horse race.

The pure truth is that the soldiers are run down by this drawn out war. There is, however, no mood of defeatism. On the contrary, there is a great frustration that we appear to have lost the war just when it seemed we were victorious. Among the troops, there is, currently, an exaggerated power of imagination. Fantasy soars. They see the ever angry, sullen face of Stalin suddenly radiating forth. He takes his fingers and draws out his long mustaches, like whips, and laughs at us. He laughs a broken, spasmodic laughter that resonates throughout the valley at the foot of the gigantic mountains.

Meanwhile, one after another, strategic points are being evacuated. He who has not witnessed the retreat of the American soldiers in Korea, who has not seen the thousands of tired, exhausted, embittered troops driving by in their trucks, has missed the true drama of the experience.

On the day of our vast evacuation, I had gone into the lounge where the chaplains would gather. As I entered, a chaplain was conversing with another on the telephone. I took no active interest in the content, but I could not help hearing snatches of the conversation. This chaplain was informing another that we were leaving the city. Suddenly, a third chaplain, who had just returned from the battlefield and who also had heard the above, sprang to his feet in anger. He grabbed the receiver from the hand of the speaker, crying, "you fool! What is the matter with you? Don't you know the Chinese are listening to our telephone communications?"

He quickly explained the source of his fury and of his warning. Just a day earlier, a Chinese, speaking fluent English, telephoned, asking when we intend to leave the city. He presented himself as an officer who merely wished to know when he should start packing. Intelligence soon learned of this trick and issued a warning to exert care with respect to telephone conversations. It was on the background of this incident that this Catholic chaplain, only recently emerged from the fire, jumped up when he heard the casual telephone talk concerning our leaving. He added, in his high hoarse voice, "you tell no one that we are evacuating. Keep all orders and rumors to yourselves. The lives of thousands of soldiers could depend upon your words or your silence."

It is difficult from afar to imagine the enormous confusion that characterized the retreat from the area of the River Yalu. When our American soldiers first closed in on the Yalu, they had the firm impression that they would have it a little easier, at least by wartime standards. Some suggested they could toss in a net and gather fish. At least they planned on a drink of fresh water, as opposed to the tepid, stale water in their canteens. In fact, why not take a bath?

But our troops expressed their good humor under an umbrella of delusion. No sooner had they arrived at the Yalu, than they had to turn around and hasten back in the direction from which they had come, but this time, through fire and flame. They retreated in indescribable disorder. It was a matter of running for one's life.

In times of great danger, a person has one desire, to maintain his own little portion of life, even if it is unbearable. In the tumult of the rout, everyone wanted simply to save himself from the Chinese. The escaping men knew that their comrades were falling all about them, but there was no looking behind or listening to the pained cries of the wounded.

How could everything have changed so lightning fast? We had all just been assured that we would be home by the Christmas holidays and that war would be a thing of the past.

I have seen the faces of those who succeeded in escaping from the furnace. I have seen the faces of the men in the white, dust-coated jeeps, and I say, without exaggeration, that the dust on their faces was as thick as that on the crooked stone roads of Korea. Their faces were masks. Only the pupils of the eyes were visible. These soldiers looked like ghosts, or like dead men. They lay, more or less in piles, one on the other, on the dusty jeeps and trucks, like bodies without souls.

One who has lived through these scenes cannot blame the soldiers for their crestfallen attitude, for their defeated demeanor. One can have no complaint against men who have fought so bitterly for their conquest, only to give back that which constituted their victories. Now, does it mean that they must go back along the same path? Few will wish to return that way, through all that hell fire.

Anywhere. The tired, exhausted soldier was prepared to go anywhere, to Europe, to Africa, to Australia, even to China, but not again through the long difficult way around to the Yalu River. It is not even a river; rather, it is a deep, accursed well, from which, as if from a secret cavern, hundreds of thousands of Chinese crawl out, their trumpets screaming out their resounding long bursts and their wild varied staccato bursts, deafening the ears and confusing the mind.

And the dust, which rises like a cloud from the countless, oncoming Chinese troops, extinguishes all light from the eyes and turns the world into darkness. The single wish is to run, to run as far as possible from the danger, to run wherever the eyes may lead one, just to live, to see once again the beauty of the world.

The soldiers, who have emerged whole from this valley of death struggle, must repeatedly recount their experiences for those curious, uninitiated who wish to hear the horror stories.

Meanwhile, I noticed that in our camps there is constant new construction, as if we were to be here a very long time. We do not know how long we are destined to remain in this area. We do know, however, that General Almond has arrived. His supervision is evident in every corner. Literally overnight everything important has been constructed, modern facilities for the troops, facilities that serve simply for their elementary needs.

The General was in an exalted mood. It was two days after Christmas. Everyone at headquarters wondered what the source of his happy mood might be. Had we driven the Chinese back to the river? Had a surprise victory occurred? No. The Colonel chaplain informed me that the reason for the General's buoyant attitude was the fact that President Truman had sent him a greeting in which the President stated that the best Christmas present he had received was the news that the Tenth Corps, officers and men, had all been evacuated from Hungnam.

In deep darkness, a drop of light is a great encouragement. Today, we hear no more of great victories, only of large, successful evacuations. How discouraging must such news be to the American at home.

But this is the picture of the situation in Korea, this far off land enveloped in the flames of war, this land that is now the center of attention for the whole mixed-up world.

Der Morgen Zhornal, January 26, 1951

The Korean War on Sea and Land

by Chaplain Milton J. Rosen

The ship that saved us from the hell of Hungnam took its time on its voyage over the sea. The Captain had seen to it that the trip would take longer, seeking various alternative routes. The Sea of Japan was tempestuous, the waves turbulent. The winds were blowing, but the ship sailed slowly and with care because it was necessary to watch out for mines, which filled these waters.

Finally, we arrived in Pusan, back to the same harbor, to which the first ships carrying U.N. soldiers came, to defend the South Koreans against the attacking North Koreans. A few hours before the landing on the coast the soldiers were in a happy mood. They felt like heroes, and when the ship dropped anchor, they were in haste to debark. The desire was not, however, very promptly realized. The ship arrived on a Monday afternoon, but the small harbor was already packed with ships, and because of the crowded conditions, we had to wait until Tuesday morning to leave.

We felt sure we could expect to stay in Pusan for a prolonged period of time. There, we could catch our breath a bit. We would no longer be stuck in a wilderness. In Pusan, life for the military was quite as comfortable as in Yokohama or Tokyo. Our certainty in this regard did not last very long, however. No sooner had we descended from the ship than we received the news that we would travel another seventy miles to the north of Pusan. We were crestfallen at this news. We had so hoped, in Pusan, once again to live as human beings. At least in Pusan, one could take a shower, go to a movie, buy something in the PX. One can even sleep in a warm room and one can walk the streets and feel one is in a city among other city dwellers.

My silent complaints and the quiet protests of the soldiers had no effect, however. It was an order, and orders were to be obeyed. Before long, we were once again standing with bag and baggage, preparing to board a train. There was an atmosphere of haste. In the rush to get situated on the train I injured my right foot. I still tend to limp. No one is paying any heed, of course. Everyone has his own troubles. In the army, one must be rather ill to warrant attention.

Koreans, strapped up like horses to narrow little wagons, carry our baggage to the station. I give my bearer a few cigarettes and get into the train, which in my view, appears to be not of the worst. Although the windowpanes are knocked out, the cars are tidy.

Inside, in the first car, stands a girl in an army uniform, and on her cap is the insignia "Red Cross." She is handing out coffee and doughnuts. With the first sips one feels immediately refreshed. We have had no breakfast. Meanwhile, the windows of all the cars are suddenly attacked by Korean children, selling all kinds of merchandise. They all know one word, "okay," but with this expression, they manage to convey the worth of their wares. A boy, about ten, comes up to the window with a beer, real American beer, which he probably bought from an American soldier for a dozen eggs. The youngster wants a whole dollar for his beer, not a penny less, or if you give him two packs of cigarettes, he will also be satisfied. Another important item in the Korean market is chewing gum. The chewing gum is such an important article of merchandise here that a five-cent pack has the value of three packs of American cigarettes. Also widespread here is the sale of pretty red apples. Indeed, the soldiers do buy these apples, in exchange for candy, cigarettes, and chewing gum, which cost the troops nothing. They are issued these items as part of their rations. Only those soldiers stationed in the big cities, such as Pusan, must buy what they want at the PX. Those assigned to front line positions receive these things every evening, at no cost, when they leave the mess hall. The prudent soldier saves up these articles for a later exchange business with Korean merchants.

Finally, the train gives a weak lurch, and we begin to travel. Everyone regrets we did not have the opportunity to stop at Pusan.

Who knows to what hidden region they will carry us off this time. Meanwhile, the stomach craves food. It is already 12:00 p.m., but as far as we can tell, no one has started to arrange for our meal. In order to fight the hunger, a group of officers has fallen upon an idea. They sit down in the middle of the train and begin to sing. Now, the aisles are replete with officers, and a song is heard throughout the cars. One hears the melodic strains of "Beautiful, Beautiful Texas." These nostalgic sounds have never had more meaning than now, on this train in Korea, so far from one's beloved homeland.

The train has been traveling high in the mountains, over snowy twisting pathways, and also in the low land, through dark tunnels. After four hours, we arrive at a station, where on a large poster is written "King George." The depot is an attractive modern building. We look about. We are seventy miles from Pusan. We have arrived at the designated point. The city opposite the depot is pretty. About forty thousand Koreans live there. The truth is, the Americans are here for the first time. One recognizes this in the clamor among the inhabitants. They hurry. They hustle. They rush to build a row of stores to get rich from their American clientele. The arrival of our soldiers has brought a festive spirit to the city.

For strategic reasons our camps are established in a mountainous region. The mountains that surround us are bleak and bare. One does not even see a memory of a tree or a plant. A powerful loneliness overcomes us as we look at our surroundings. It feels as if one were placed in an endless fantasy imprisonment, with high, solid walls through which one could not break. But, in the Army everything is done quickly, in a spirit of great haste. Before one looks around, he finds himself ensconced in a room in a school building. A stove has been placed for heating. This room will be the office for six chaplains, three Catholic, two Protestant and one Jewish. Here we should have comfortable lodging. In addition to the chaplains, three soldiers will make their home here—assistants.

The first night we are all tired and worn out and go to sleep early. I am having difficulty with my foot. The pain is severe, and it is difficult to step on it. Nevertheless, I do what the others do. I get into my sleeping bag and soon fall asleep.

Suddenly, in the middle of the night, I hear, as if in a dream, an outcry, "Fire! Fire!" I get up and look out my window. It is indeed no dream. A real fire is blazing. The house opposite us is enveloped in flame. The strong winds are blowing the fire in the direction of our building. The sparks are already falling upon our roof. I wake up my roommates, and soon we are all outside, in the field, where the winter cold rages from all sides. In spite of the panic, we have managed to pull out all of our things. The fire encompasses all the walls of the three-storied building. We stand helpless, freezing in the extremely cold night.

Only after a half hour do the Korean firemen appear with their old-fashioned fire apparatus. There is a great racket, a turmoil. One fireman steps over a second fireman. Wild shouting comes through the night air. The fire grows worse, but the fire personnel are occupied with their hollering. Everyone is nervous. Finally, thank Heaven, the fire hoses have been brought out and are available to attack the flames. The firemen hold the hose in the direction of the flaming building, but no water emerges. What has happened? We start to look at the rubbery hoses. The pump is working, water seems to fill, but suddenly we note that the water is running out through the near end of the hose. The hose is not tightly screwed into the water source, and the water pours out of the source onto the field. The racket goes on. The arguments grow more intense. Confusion embraces everyone. Time continues to pass, and the fire blows about ever more intensely. The firemen stand, holding their hoses, and while the building burns, bicker on.

All night, work goes on with the fire apparatus until the fire is finally contained, and the spread to the surrounding area avoided, and in the morning the damage is assessed. It turns out that the government has had a bit of luck. The damages for the building amount to no more than $70,000. This is, of course, not to consider the untold thousands it would cost to replace the incinerated Army materiel that could not be saved.

Der Morgen Zhornal, January 29, 1951

Jewish Soldiers in Korea Long for Traditional Judaism

by Chaplain Milton J. Rosen

On a dark night during which the echo of distant cannon fire spreads over our camps, which lie at the foot of the massive mountains, I think that not one of the Jewish fathers and mothers, grandparents, relatives, or friends would really want to know what is going on with their son, grandson, or dear one of any status, stationed in the regions of the battles in Korea.

I think that what they really want to know is what their loved ones may be doing behind the front lines, how they spend their free time after the daily routine, and, in essence, whether they have remained the Jewish children they knew.

It would be a mistake to believe that the Jewish boys, who at home were no religious zealots, would suddenly, here near the front, turn penitent and devote body and soul to Judaism. On the other hand, one can discern a certain alteration in mentality of some of these very soldiers. On the basis of my observations, I have arrived at the conclusion that some Jewish youngsters who had not wanted to be bound by Jewish observance and who had never wanted to set foot in a synagogue, have now, suddenly, under the influence of their experiences, become rather different people. One could postulate that the reason for this sudden transformation is their loneliness, their separation from home by thousands of miles, but whatever the source, the fact is they are beginning, gradually, to return to Jewish practice. A sort of inexplicable yearning prods them back to Jewish tradition, to draw faith and courage from the Jewish religion. The best proof of this is the Friday night religious service, which is so strongly attended by those apparently estranged Jewish youth.

In connection with this, it may be appropriate to recount an episode, which on the surface might sound a bit peculiar, but which, at the same time, can give one an insight into the manner in which a Jewish boy, far from the practice of Judaism, could suddenly become a staunch member of my congregation.

While still in Japan, in Yokohama, when I would come to my chapel each

Friday for Friday night services, I noted there was, at times, a young man in uniform who would sneak in during the services, always late. At the end of the religious ceremonies, however, he was generally first to the dining table. The Japanese serving girl who waited the table was somewhat astounded by his behavior. The tasty dishes that were offered rendered him unable to sit still. He would fill his plate with cold fish, eating with such appetite, as if he had undergone a fast of months. He would drink wine in place of water, and by the time the other soldiers would sit down to the table, the bottle was nearly empty. He would first drink the wine of sanctification of the Sabbath, then drink to toast the happy occasion, and thereafter, fulfilled in advance the commandment of the four cups of wine of the Passover Seder. He relished it all and would gasp, "Oh, this is good!" For his fellow soldiers, all that would be left would be to utter the toast of "L'chaim," over the remnants. No nut was left untouched, no raisin untasted, no peas untried. His eyes, however, were cast, in particular, toward the matzos—not, Heaven forbid, a few matzos, but rather, the whole box of matzos. He was a passionate eater of matzos.

This young man behaved in this fashion every Friday night he attended. He overindulged the wine, stuffed himself with matzos, and with a heart full of good will, began talking with those around the table. He did not lack for listeners. His audience consisted of men and women, soldiers and civilians.

He was a hearty conversationalist, and the assembled listened to him with great interest. He spoke with fire and flare about virtually every subject, but he would persistently avoid religion. He never wanted to discuss the issue. If someone would bring up religious problems with a view to hearing his opinion, he would turn pale, give evasive answers, stammer in a manner indicative of his discomfort, and if pressed further, would seek a door with which to escape. Once, when he found himself in just such a situation, he grabbed a near empty box of matzos, poured the remnants into his hand, then stuffed them like peanuts into his pockets, and left.

When I stopped him once, as he was departing at the door, I asked him if he was so very "busy" that he had to leave early. He replied that he was indeed not busy, but when the subject of religion would come up, he felt nervous and tired and had the need to go home to bed. I asked a few more questions, resulting in his open admission that he had no interest in the story of Passover or the chicken dumplings. He just happened to love matzos, which is why he showed up on Friday nights. He also told me his father had given him some instruction in Judaism, but that it was not very extensive.

Hearing this I went into the kitchen and came out with a whole box of matzos, which I gave him. I also gave him a packet of pamphlets on the subject of Judaism and a copy of the Jewish Bible, and I suggested that whenever he ate the matzos, he might also look at the words of this small treasure I had given him. He smiled, thanked me, and left. Well, what does the Talmud say? "A mountain will not encounter another mountain, but a man will indeed meet another man." When, in the recent past, I arrived in Hamhung, Korea, whom did I meet? The first Jewish soldier I encountered was this same young man—the matzo eater. As soon as he saw me, he became animated, crying out with unrestrained joy, "Chaplain, I'm so happy to see you! Now, we'll eat matzos again!" When, some days later, it became necessary to leave Hamhung for the harbor city, he was the first member of my new congregation. He became active in seeking out other Jewish soldiers who wanted to become members of the congregation. One could soon observe the results of his efforts. Indeed, the first Friday night I had a handsome number of congregants.

My matzo lover could virtually never get enough of this unleavened Passover bread, which our ancestors had baked in such haste in the desert. He ate and sighed in pleasure. It seemed that every sigh cost me a matzo, but I did notice that, in addition to matzos, he was now devoted to prayers. He told me that since we had last seen each other, he had begun to read a lot about Judaism and was grateful for my stimulus in this regard. This same soldier, who had now returned to his faith, was also a frequent visitor to my chapel in Kyongju, where currently bitter battles are being fought. We had by that time become fast friends.

His efforts on behalf of the congregation continued to intensify. Once, however, his persistent addiction to matzos got him into serious trouble. It was his nightly habit to place a box of matzos near his bed, so that he could grab a piece of matzo on awakening. One night, after he had fallen asleep, a piece of matzo in his mouth, a number of rats entered his bungalow and began to chew his matzos with gusto at his bedside. While it is not unusual for the Korean rats to be guests whenever there is food, their presence over his bedding apparently was a stimulus for a singular dream in which Chinese soldiers had stealthily crept into the bungalow, approaching the sleeping American soldiers, step by step, bayonets fixed, prepared to slaughter. Still half asleep, our soldier grabbed a rifle and nearly began to shoot in the direction of the matzos-devouring rats. Another soldier, whose bed was opposite, awoke from the racket, noted his comrade jumping about, hollering, and aiming his rifle, regarded him as having gone mad and screamed, "What are you doing, Soldier?"

At this, our friend awoke fully from his dream and recognized the intruders to be Korean rats, not Chinese soldiers. He was most grateful to his neighbor, whose timely cry probably prevented a catastrophe. He realized he could have shot a fellow soldier. From that time on, he brought no matzos into his quarters. The soldier's name is Abe Silverman, and he wishes, through my offices, to send greetings to his parents, Jack and Baileh Silverman, 545 Powell Street, Brooklyn. He also wants to inform his parents that he, previously an accountant in Brooklyn, also works here in Korea, in the finance office, and is in the best of health.

Der Morgen Zhornal, February 1, 1951

A New York Theological Student and Other Jewish Soldiers at the Korean Front

Chanukah Candles in a Military Hospital in Korea

by Chaplain Milton J. Rosen

It was only a few days before Chanukah when I arrived in Hamhung. As I stepped into my headquarters I was aware of the heavy odor of gunpowder in the air. The imminent danger was creeping over our heads. We had prepared thoroughly for the evacuation of the city. The enemy was moving ever closer, and we sensed the very echo of his footsteps.

I have attempted in earlier articles to portray the circumstances in which we found ourselves as the enemy approached. I have described the ominous character of the situation. The city was nearly empty. No one was traveling over the streets, and certainly, no one was traveling outside the city. There were even rumors that the Chinese had infiltrated the city, in disguise. The urgency to evacuate intensified. However, there was a lack of transportation. My office had been allotted three jeeps, and there were five chaplains. I wanted very much to visit a hospital some distance from the city. I wanted to celebrate the holiday of Chanukah with the Jewish soldiers there, but it was difficult to find a jeep. This holiday, recalling the victory of the Maccabees in ancient Israel,[1] is a national Jewish holiday of great importance, and I regard it as equally important that our soldiers, who fight now for freedom in a far away foreign land, should indeed celebrate the day commemorating the Jewish War of Liberation, fought thousands of years ago. I stood at the appropriate road, scratching my brow, perplexed. How could I acquire a car, a truck, a jeep? I was willing to accept a horse and buggy if such had been available.

To those who do not share my background, it would be difficult to understand the urgency I felt to make this visit. Aside from the holiday, which is very important to us, there is the issue of "Bikur Cholim," the obligation to visit the sick, and there is the commandment incumbent on us, "These are the precepts for which no fixed measure is ordained."[2] In any case, I could not get a jeep released to me, as there were other matters being pursued by the other chaplains.

As I sat in my office, continuing to worry about the problem of getting to the hospital and the Jewish soldiers, a tall, blond soldier came into the office, carrying a document requiring the signature of the Colonel chaplain. Before he left the room, I noted him staring at the Jewish chaplain's insignia attached to my uniform. I stared at him, in return. The whole incident lasted only a few seconds. In my view, he appeared to be 100 percent Swedish, having a look about him of the cold far North. There was certainly nothing in his expression to suggest a Jewish stereotype. He remained at the door, listening attentively as I again spoke with the chaplains about the issue of the jeep. He seemed thoughtful. Finally, he turned and disappeared, without a word.

A half hour later, the blond soldier reappeared. He danced into the room, out of breath, his coat thrown over his shoulders. He strode over to me with nimble steps and with a resounding voice announced, "Okay, Chaplain. Come on. We're going to the hospital." "And how are we going to get to the hospital?" I asked. "I have a jeep for you," he replied. I was a bit puzzled by this sudden kind offer. What was the reason for this friendliness? In any case, his offer came as a salvation from Heaven, and I asked no further questions. I immediately took my seat in the jeep and we were off. At the wheel, he told me he had to travel in this direction anyway and would drop me at the hospital.

As we emerged onto the wider, open road, the soldier suddenly drew forth a grenade from his pocket. He bit off the pin as one might bite the stem from our traditional lemon-like *esrog*, and as if from thin air, begin to speak to me in a beautiful Yiddish. I was astounded to hear his language. This was no Americanized Yiddish, which contains 60 percent English and only 40 percent Yiddish. It contained no slang. It was really a literary Yiddish, official, as it was meant to be, with all the catchwords, aphorisms, witticisms, and intonations. He quoted Morris Rosenfeld and Sholem Aleichem and even our writers of *Der Morgen Zhornal.*

Hearing this, my spirits lightened and I exclaimed, "Is this true? Are you Jewish?" "Am I Jewish?" he replied. "I am a Yeshiva boy, a Jewish theological student! My name is Nathan David Reznick. I was a student at the Tiferet Jerusalem Theological School founded in large part by my grandfather, Rabbi Isar Reznick."

I was now truly curious regarding this young man and wanted to learn more about him and his background. He told me his father ran a factory, located on Canal Street in New York City, making men's working aprons. His name was Mordecai Reznick.

Gradually, my companion began to reveal bits of his philosophy of life. According to his manner, he appeared to take a negative view toward war. He didn't seem strongly inclined to carry a rifle, even when traveling outside the city. He had, however, his reasons and began to lecture me in weapons' tactics, whereby I began to understand his preference for a grenade over a rifle.

He explained that when a soldier travels on an open road in Korea and a bullet suddenly appears to be coming in his direction, he may be quite certain that some Chinese soldier is shooting at him from his hiding place. In that circumstance, there is little time to reach for a rifle, seek out the place of origin of the enemy fire and then hit the appropriate target. With a grenade in his hand, however, the defender can toss it quickly in the direction of the enemy fire and be reasonably certain the shooter will not emerge alive. This was not hearsay on his part. It was based on his own experience.

The jeep appeared to gallop over the open road, my soldier friend driving purposefully, while maintaining a stream of quotations from Talmudic Sages, traditional expositions of the Torah, and sharp-witted Yiddish jokes in excellent Yiddish. He knew the "Sayings of the Fathers" by heart. Wherever he went, he maintained the daily practice of putting on the ritual phylacteries and praying the prescribed three times a day. War is war, but to abandon his devotion to Judaism because of it was not appropriate. On the contrary, my articulate companion concluded that in time of danger, one must apply himself all the more.

When we stopped at the hospital entrance, we could already perceive a racket from within. All the Jewish soldiers were assembled, impatiently waiting for the lighting of the Chanukah candles, which represent the wonders of an ancient time and the strength of the Jewish people in those days, when a venerable nation fought for freedom and defeated their enemy. I was soon surrounded by soldiers, with affection and regard. Among them was a young man named Garson Goodman, a fine cantor, who, because of his musical talents had taken over the role of chaplain among the Marines.

During this happy, noisy time, we lit the Chanukah candles and sang "Rock of Ages." The flames of the small candles illuminated the walls and the faces of the men and brought forth a very special festive spirit among these wounded Jewish soldiers. The small fires were as torches, the flames flickering upward. The men sang louder, and higher, and from their song arose not only the melodic strains of these American soldiers but also those of the ancient Maccabees.

I was very moved. As I listened to their resounding song, my heart was full of joy. We are everywhere. We take part in every war of liberation. Korea is no exception. And this is our army in Korea, where Jewish heroes do their part in the war for freedom.

Der Morgen Zhornal, February 6, 1951

Jewish Soldiers in Korea Who Long for a Synagogue and Judaism

Jewish Soldiers Who Have Abandoned Their Judaism

by Chaplain Milton J. Rosen

A Jewish chaplain, who must seek out the Jewish soldiers behind the front lines, is comparable to a shepherd who must keep a watchful eye on his flock, spread about in all directions.

As Jewish chaplain, it is my duty, as far as possible, to visit Jewish soldiers wherever they may be found, even to the farthest posts. It is not the easiest task, but it needs to be done. It is not as much a problem for chaplains of other religions. Most of those chaplains are attached to a battalion, and not seldom, even to an entire regiment. They need not seek members for their congregations. All they need do is announce the time and the place of their worship services, and an audience is assured. Of five hundred men, these chaplains will have at least seventy or eighty attendees. It may not be proportionately a very large number, but it is not necessary to search for them with a candle.

In our situation, the issue is rather different. Our soldiers do not always run at first call to the Service of the Creator. I sometimes have the feeling that a Jewish chaplain could sound trumpets over the whole camp to no avail. There are various reasons for this. First of all, it is the question of whether there are any Jewish troops in the area. Secondly, one must admit that there are in every camp soldiers who wait to be personally invited. They appear to expect the chaplain to find them in the most remote military quarters.

This does not, Heaven forbid, apply to the Jewish soldiers in general. One must emphasize that many, finding themselves away from home, are most enthusiastic to hear their Jewish chaplain. They come on their own, and they bring along other lost sheep. Nevertheless, the task of seeking out the Jewish boys, distributed over various areas, remains the main obligation of the chaplain. He must leave his own space and undertake his travels throughout the scattered camps. When, in the course of his wanderings, he comes upon a needy Jewish soldier, it is as if he has been guided by a true saving angel.

How one finds these stray Jewish boys is a chapter in itself. It would, also, be appropriate to mention that in the chaplain's quest, he is not always alone. Often he is assisted by Christian chaplains, who consider it a good deed to help find the Jewish soldiers. They have their own ways and means of detection and seem to possess a keen talent at scenting the whereabouts of the Jewish troops, whereupon they give the names over to their Jewish colleague and provide him access to his Jewish brothers throughout the camps. He is then able to gather them together under one roof to hear God's word. On the basis of my experience, I have, however, come to the conclusion that not all the Jewish boys wait impatiently for the advent of the chaplain's visit. It is notable how busy some soldiers become when convinced that the chaplain has appeared in their section.

The Jewish chaplain must be adept at luring the soldier. He must himself be an attraction. He simply cannot suddenly descend from heaven. He must apply various methods to awaken the interest of the soldier, whose heart and ears he seeks. He must know what to say and what not to say. He must not immediately launch into a discussion of religion or serving the will of the Creator. He must first earn his friendship. He must have the sensitivity of the detective. He must feel the pulse of each soldier. He must ascertain the tastes of the other. Does he like an orthodox rabbi or a conservative rabbi? The chaplain must also determine what kind of upbringing his soldier received at home. In order to do this, one must initiate irrelevant conversation and innocent talk. It does not hurt to include a few jokes, a sharp witticism. One becomes a good brother, one finds out about his parents, about his environment, about his needs, and when one has won his trust, he becomes a friend, and indeed, a devoted friend. Be he a Reform Jew and you an Orthodox Rabbi, the rupture from his home environment brings him close to you. The great distance has a powerful effect on people seeking friendship far from home.

It is superfluous to say that those Jewish soldiers who have received a fundamentally Jewish upbringing at home do not require the kind of methodology mentioned above to bring them close to the chaplain. It is a fact, however, that a considerable number of Jewish soldiers, for various reasons concerning which I do not wish to speak here, deny that they are Jews. Often, there results from this issue great unpleasantness. I have much to say regarding this tragedy, but let this one example suffice for the moment, to give a real picture of the situation.

About two years ago, when I was a chaplain in Japan, there used to come to my chapel a soldier, about forty years of age. He had already served in the Army some eighteen years, but he had never risen higher than the rank of corporal. Although I do not believe in the stereotypical physical characteristics of Jews, there was something in the appearance of this Jewish corporal that appealed to me as being very Jewish, something that set him apart from those around him. Also, in his mentality, he seemed thoroughly Jewish. In his conversations he would throw in a few succulent Jewish expressions, fresh from Delancy Street and Clinton Street in New York.

He would come to my chapel and invite himself into my kitchen for coffee. He would speak of the gefilte fish and dumplings that his mother used to make for him. On Friday night or on Festival nights, however, he would not appear, for which he had plenty of excuses. During the week, he would bring his "oksan" with him, the small, thin Japanese woman whom he hoped one day to bring to America. He complained of her lack of cleverness, however, in not being able to speak a word of Yiddish. His friendship with this "oksan" was difficult for me to understand. On one occasion, he would groan over her. The next time, he would, with delight, call her his "babysan."

The real surprise was brought to me by this young man precisely on Yom Kippur eve.[3] All over the land of Japan, Jewish soldiers and Jewish civilians were preparing themselves to go to the chapel for the solemn "Kol Nidre."[4] Everyone in the Army knew that the fearful day had come. All day long the chaplain was busy answering when and where the services would be held. Soon, the last hour had arrived. The sun was setting in the west and the public streamed to "Kol Nidre." Suddenly the telephone rang. I grabbed the receiver. The hoarse voice of the soldier with the "oksan" was speaking, saying he was in deep trouble. He had asked his captain for leave for the next day so that he could go to the synagogue. Aside from the fact that this was the Yom Kippur holiday, this day would also be the date of his mother's memorial,[5] the date of the passing of the very same mother whose dumplings and gefilte fish he praised so much in his conversations with me. He wanted to come to the synagogue to say the memorial prayer for her, but the captain did not want to hear about it. The young man sobbed over the phone like a child, begging that I should beseech this captain to allow him to attend memorial services for his mother.

I immediately called the strict captain who would prohibit this Jewish, albeit estranged, soldier from going to the synagogue on Yom Kippur. However, this captain answered me in a most polite manner, stating that this soldier happens to be a devout Catholic in every sense, and according to his knowledge of him, this soldier is simply a lazy idler who does not want to work, but does like to dance at weddings. I argue that he is a bona fide Jew. I was not at his circumcision, but I know him well from our frequent meetings. The captain was disappointed at my naiveté. How skillfully had this soldier fooled me. He had before him the man's record! This soldier had always claimed to be a pure Catholic, and if I still doubt his findings, I could call the colonel.

It is superfluous to say that I soon got the colonel on the line. He offered me a "shalom aleichem"[6] in tasteful Hebrew. We conversed informally and in an atmosphere of camaraderie about the lot of the soldier who wanted to observe the memorial service in the synagogue. The colonel agreed to look into the record and call me right back. I was already tense over the issue. Was it possible? A Catholic who spoke Yiddish from Delancy Street and Clinton Street? The telephone soon rang, however, and the Jewish colonel answered that he too, was surprised to learn that in the record of this soldier, it was clearly stated black on white that he is a Catholic.

I was perplexed. It was nearly the time for Yom Kippur. The chapel was already full of soldiers, and here I was, full of doubt, about a person who cries that he is Jewish and must say the memorial service for his mother. It occurred to me to put the following argument to the colonel: Why should not this man be permitted to go to the synagogue on the day of Yom Kippur to say the memorial service, even if we both have doubts concerning his Jewish origin. After all, this soldier at this time is not interested in himself, but in his mother's soul. If he was indeed Jewish, but had, because of personal, perhaps practical reasons, purported to be Catholic, he would have, in any case, because of his actions, brought grief to his mother, who had certainly already suffered sufficiently from her son, while still alive.

In short, a conversation here, a discussion there, we came to a solution. If the young man would promise to go to the synagogue tomorrow and pray the whole day, as a true Jew must, the colonel would forgive his previous fabrications and would state in the record that he is Jewish, and that would be that.

He was called by the colonel and did indeed attend the synagogue. His Japanese girlfriend, the "oksan," came along as well. She stood all day in the back section, somewhat confused, but beamed with pride over her young man, who had become a full fledged, hundred percent Jew, at least for this day.

Der Morgen Zhornal, February 8, 1951

Jewish Soldiers in Korea Send Greetings to Their Parents through the Chaplain

A Soldier Who Tried to Flee from His People

by Chaplain Milton J. Rosen

A Jewish chaplain in Korea will not seldom encounter bizarre events. Things and happenings that appear unusual or even astounding in the daily civilian life are quite normal in life behind the front lines.

I speak of this in connection with another case of a Jewish youth, wearing a soldier's uniform in Korea, who had tried for a long time to disclaim his Jewish tradition. The Jewishness in him, however, would not abandon him. It came to him in a dream and told him he should not run away from himself. Following this, our soldier did not require that anyone interpret this message. He understood well the significance of this nocturnal vision and, on his own, recognized his Jewish identity once again. The story is as follows: When I came to this camp, I sought out all of the Jewish soldiers. I recognized my Jewish boys at first sight. I had no difficulty establishing a relationship with any one of them, except for one young man, with a genuine Jewish surname, who denied being Jewish. I was not alone in my conviction that he was a brother Israelite. All the Jewish soldiers gave their testimony that he was certainly Jewish.

It should be understood that I did not, Heaven forbid, pose questions to him regarding religion, in spite of the fact that upon our introduction to each other, his name and impression were patently Jewish. I did ask a favor of him, however; namely, that if he happened to encounter a Jewish soldier in his tent, he might be so kind as to inform him that Jewish services were being held in camp. The youth answered with a smile, "yes sir!" and was away. As it happened, his neighbor in the same tent was a Jewish soldier who tended to visit me often.

The latter, on one occasion, came in and told me that the previous night, when he was enjoying a sound sleep in his tent, he was suddenly awakened by a strange noise. He sat up in bed, hastily, and listened. What did he hear? His Jewish neighbor, who denied his background, had cried out in his sleep, but not only cried out, he was carrying on a conversation in loud tones. He hollered so loudly that one could hear precisely what he was saying. He was speaking in genuine Yiddish about something to do with a rabbi and a synagogue. According to the choppy discussion he was having with himself, one could discern that a rabbi was pressing him to attend synagogue, which he did not want to do, and he was defending himself constantly with a cry, "I don't want to go to the synagogue, and you can't force me to!"

The soldier who related this to me smiled at his little victory. "Now he cannot deny that he is Jewish. He has just admitted it on his own." I too was under the impression that this soldier's Jewish conscience was crying out during his sleep. I did nothing. I waited, patiently, for the reaction of this young man, who had been running from himself. I did not need to wait long. Only a few days later, on a beautiful, cold afternoon, the dreamer came to my cabin and with an abashed smile, apologized for not having come to services until now. He confessed that his conscience had been plaguing him the entire time. He had been suffering from a conflict, and deep within him regretted that he had consistently hidden his Jewishness. My innocent mention that he might send Jewish boys to the services had finally aroused in him a deep remorse. My words seemed to remain strongly invested in his memory, which circumstance appears to have led to his unusual dream involving strife with a rabbi who wanted him to attend synagogue. The dream, in his view, drew him instantly from his previous behavior.

After this confession, that which followed went like a song. He told me that he is from a fine, orthodox family. The rabbi of his city had indeed taught him. He had even become a candidate to study at a Jewish theological school and had ambition to become a rabbi, but military service had intervened. The war, the loneliness of military duty, the nostalgia day and night while in the camps, torn away from home and family, had driven him to run from himself. Now, it is as if he has acquired a new being. He has fully awakened. He is once again cheerful and lively. He belongs somewhere. He feels he has roots. He has found himself once again and will never again in his life deny who he is.

This episode characterizes only a certain element among the Jewish soldiers, who labor under an inferiority complex, when it comes to revealing themselves. In general, however, on my journeys, I meet Jewish soldiers who declare themselves with great enthusiasm as Jews and indeed as Jews who carry their Judaism with pride.

On one of my recent trips from camp to camp, I stopped off at the headquarters of the Seventh Division. There, there was simply a multitude of Jewish soldiers. I quickly gathered them together in an army tent where we prayed the afternoon prayer of "Mincha." Afterwards we talked together until it was time for the evening prayer of "Maariv." After "Maariv," I arranged a supper of Jewish dishes—gefilte fish, matzos, wine, and other delicacies. It sometimes happens that the "Chief Wine Steward,"[7] namely, the cook in charge, is also Jewish. He brewed coffee for us. We visited together in a warm and happy mood until late at night. In a second camp, not far away, the scenario was much the same.

In most camps, there is joy and happiness at a visit from the Jewish chaplain. Through the chaplain, the Jewish soldiers acquire a direct connection with home, with their parents, who are thousands of miles away. The chaplain is actually the communications man between the soldier at the front and the family at home. The soldiers use my presence effectively, sending through me lively greetings to their loved ones.

At this point, I gladly undertake the role of messenger of good deeds and record the names of Jewish boys in Uncle Sam's Army who send their greetings directly from Korea to their parents in America: Captain, MD, Stanley D. Levitas, of 432 Ellsworth Avenue, New Haven, Connecticut; Captain (dentist) Sheldon Koltof, of 1756 East Madison Street, Philadelphia, Pennsylvania; Saul Djerling, from Brooklyn; Stanley Eisenberg, 2840 Ocean Avenue, of Brooklyn, New York; Isador Seidenberg, 1537 Araby, San Pedro, California; Corporal Allan P. Goldman, 1304 Marion Avenue, Bronx, New York; John Behr, who is proud of the three years he spent at Columbia College, and who was also in the last war, having come to America in 1932 from Nuremberg, sending greetings to his father and mother in New York; Private Walter H. Adam, of New York; Lieutenant Emanuel Borak; Private Ralph Schlesinger, of New York; Private N. Goldberg, of St. Louis, Missouri; Joseph Ronnel of New York. They all send their greetings to their parents and relatives.[8]

I send their greetings with much pleasure, for I know that these youngsters in Korea are doing as I am doing, serving as Americans and Jews in Uncle

Sam's Army, which is waging a heroic fight to preserve freedom and equality for all the countries of the world.

Four Jewish chaplains serve in Korea, and their names are: Garson Goodman; Oscar M. Lipchitz; Joseph B. Messing, and, yours truly, Milton J. Rosen.

Der Morgen Zhornal, February 20, 1951

Director of a Jazz Band Serves as Cantor for Jewish Soldiers in Korea

Jewish Soldier, Who Escaped from the Communist Trap, Relates His Experiences

A Trip through Destroyed Cities and Towns in Korea

by Chaplain Milton J. Rosen

On one of the cold, pretty mornings, I set out on a journey that was to take me over widespread areas of Korea. The cold seemed to penetrate one's bones, but the sun shown through, with its rather spare, reluctant rays. One must not forget that in the frosty winter of South Korea, even a few cool sun rays are regarded as an immeasurable treasure.

Before my headquarters waited a jeep and driver, and to my surprise, a Catholic chaplain, who stood by the vehicle. He had intentionally, on his own, taken time off to accompany me on my trip throughout the dispersed camps where it was my custom to seek out Jewish soldiers.

This Catholic chaplain was quite prepared to help me in my work. He had even anticipated and had announced to the Jewish soldiers on a previous trip through the camps that I would be paying a visit. He even organized the sergeants of various companies to telephone the Jewish soldiers regarding my arrival.

Before I started out on this journey, I clothed myself as if I were preparing an expedition to Alaska. I wore thick clothing, my body bundled up in layer on layer. As they say in the Army, I looked like a stuffed goose. Actually, however, I did well in this regard, since the jeep had no doors, and I was sure the wind would whip in all directions. I put up my collar so that my ears would not freeze.

Suddenly I became aware that the driver of the jeep was looking at me rather sharply, and after a few seconds he told me that he remembered me from Japan, when I served there in the cold north region. Looking back at the driver, I recalled once again what a small world it is. The driver, who a few years earlier carried me over broad stretches of Japan, was now my driver on the roads of Korea.

The area through which we first had to travel was not very long, totaling only thirty-two miles. The jeep, on a good paved main road, should have been able to travel as if on a slide. Indeed, under such circumstances, if I had been sitting in a Plymouth or Chevrolet, the whole trip would not have taken more than half an hour. But try to manage that on the crippled roads of Korea! The broken thoroughfares serve as highways, as main roads, but in actuality, they are like torn up gutters. The American highways are like boulevards compared to the Korean "royal roads." It is difficult to believe that a land with a population of thirty million can exist under such primitive conditions.

With respect to open roads and transportation means, however, I have to admit that in North Korea the situation is considerably better. This is a result of the fact that in North Korea, industry simply required the paving of some first class roads. In South Korea, connecting roads were totally neglected, perhaps because South Korea is, for the most part, a land of primitive farms. A need for highways did not come to mind. For the wooden wheels that the yoked ox must pull, for the primitive old fashioned wagons bearing fruit or rice, such roads are sufficient and may be sufficient for the next century. In South Korea, one asks, "What is the hurry?" The farmer has always been poor and will remain poor.

Around us stretched the gigantic mountains. Korea is enveloped by mountains as a leprosy surrounds an afflicted body. One mountain appears to grow atop another. The eye sees only the naked rock, without traces of a leaf, a plant, a tree. Between these mighty mountains winds a thin tortuous road. The road is so narrow that if a jeep, to say nothing of a truck, is coming toward you from the opposite direction, he must squeeze you against the wall, like Balaam's ass, or you must slide off the road.

Often, traveling along these paths, one sees here and there an overturned truck or jeep. This is undoubtedly a result of an accident that occurred in the darkness of the night. As long as the world goes on wheels, one must indeed drive, and in the meantime, there is no one to whom to complain. The worst is the objects that continually fly at your head, stirred up by the rolling wheels. If one receives such a stone directly to the forehead, one sees a most brightly lit sky. The dust rises like clouds and enters your nostrils, your lungs, your innards, and you literally chew earth. The jeep shakes and heaves so mightily on all sides that your entrails also heave and your teeth knock against one another, and if it happens you have false teeth, it would be better to keep them in your pocket, lest they fall out.

If the journey had proceeded without interruption, all of the above would have been only half the aggravation. It happens, however, rather often, that suddenly, without warning, the road will be cut off and one can find himself on the pinnacle of a mountain and must slide off into a field, on occasion, into a stream or a river. In such a situation one is forced to ford that river just as was the case in ancient times at the Red Sea, only on this occasion, sitting in a jeep. One can also go astray and land in a marsh and emerge from the depths, by virtue of miracles. A passenger moans, and the driver sighs or delivers a juicy curse, after which a silence descends. The quiet does not come voluntarily. You are forced to remain silent, because if you open your mouth, waves of dirt enter your throat and bring on endless coughing.

One cannot claim that a trip over the desolate roads in Korea is entertaining. It is boring in the extreme. The only break in the monotony is due to the scenes of the small distant figures in the fields and their colorful clothing. Especially eye-catching from afar are the women with the large earthen jugs of water on their heads or the old-fashioned farmers with their tall cylindrical headgear. The elders along the way bear stately visages. They stride along proudly with a tree branch in their hand, and their narrow, tiny beards sway back and forth in the breeze as they walk.

This trip lasts an hour and forty minutes, every minute an eternity, for aside from the fear of ambush there is the fear of a bullet from the hidden guerrilla sniper. Every day we are told of several jeep drivers who have been shot by guerrillas. The Catholic chaplain who was traveling with me freely violated the Geneva Convention and without reservation carried a revolver. My concern did not diminish with this knowledge. I do not carry a handgun. First of all, I haven't taken time to acquire one and secondly, I don't know how to shoot. It appears, finally, I shall have to learn the art of maintaining a weapon. I shall have to recognize the law of war—you live by your sword. Finally, we arrived peacefully at one of the companies. There, a young Jewish soldier awaited me. He was the only Jew among several hundred Christian soldiers. When he saw me, a broad smile spread over his face. He told me he was the director of a jazz band, his work being to provide music for the morale of the troops. He seemed to me to be a David of his time, a player of the fiddle and a soldier who goes to war with his rifle.

He told me he had been in the very decisive fiery firefight in Hamhung and barely emerged alive. He is among the few survivors of the Thirty-third Army,[9] which suffered great losses. The Thirty-third Army was attacked not far from the Chosen Reservoir.

The young soldier told of striking episodes in the battle of Hamhung, episodes of fire and blood. When he finished his narration, he hospitably took out some cookies from a tin box and offered them to me. With this, he declared, "My wife sent me these. My wife keeps a kosher home."

I took out some wine from my knapsack and we toasted a "L'chaim." He showed me his prayer book and prayer shawl. He told me he served as Cantor for the Seventh Division, and as proof that he did not exaggerate, chanted for me quite spontaneously. He has a fine voice and he chants the prayers in an excellent Hebrew. He completed his rendition in a manner quite consistent with cantorial tradition.

The name of this young man is Oliver (Elijah) Margolin. He asked me to deliver greetings to his family in San Francisco, by means of *Der Morgen Zhornal.* He actually comes from New York. His uncle, Harry Leventhal, of Washington Heights, is in the pickle business. He sells his juicy pickles to the inhabitants of that great city of eight million souls—New York.

Der Morgen Zhornal, February 27, 1951

High-Ranking Jewish Officers in Korea, Estranged from Their People

Also, Many Warmly Dedicated Jewish Servicemen

A Service Where Jewish Soldiers Show Movies of the War in Israel

by Chaplain Milton J. Rosen

On my many trips to meet Jewish troops, including those made while I was still stationed in Japan, I encountered a number of unpleasant experiences. A Jewish chaplain is privileged to meet many interesting persons. I must underscore sadly that at least the majority of Jews who succeed in the Army and who manage to ascend the ladder of high office tend rapidly to forget their Jewishness.

The more successful they are the more they wish to pass for non-Jews. It is curious that no sooner do they become captains then they hide from the Jewish chaplain and avoid a Jewish environment, to say nothing of their attitude when they reach the rank of major. One cannot find them if he searches for them with a torch, and when a young Jewish man becomes a colonel he does not appear at the Seder on Passover or in the chapel on Yom Kippur.

There are a number of reasons why they conceal themselves from their Judaism. First of all, they don't consider it any longer appropriate to mix with non-officers. Secondly they fear that the non-Jews will recognize that they are Jews, and this might reduce their military status. The truth is everyone in the Army knows, in any case, that they are Jews, and this knowledge turns out to be quite useful. It has happened on many occasions, when I have searched out Jewish soldiers to determine how many matzos, approximately, I needed to prepare for Passover, that Christian officers in those places help me very effectively. They would inform me who was a Jewish colonel, major, or captain. Not seldom have my Christian friends asked me why it is that they do not see a particular Jewish officer going to chapel on Friday night.

From my experience, I know that in the Army there is actually great respect for the Jewish officer who does not hide his religion. After all, we all are in the Army for the single purpose of protecting our land and the ideals of our democracy, which preaches freedom for all religions and free choice for every sort of religious service. The true American officer has come to the understanding that any person who denies his origin, his religion, because he is afraid or ashamed, is not a real American. Yet our high-ranking Jewish officers who have worked themselves up to their elevated positions pretend not to recognize that they are brothers among the children of Israel when they see the chaplain coming.

I remember a case when in great haste I virtually grabbed a Jewish colonel by the lapel because I needed to see him regarding an issue that had to do with Army business, not Jewish affairs. This Jewish colonel was most restless. He was nervous and rattled. I had the impression that he was in dread that I might remind him concerning Passover, which was then at the threshold. He would forestall me, yet seek his security, asking me to send him some wine and matzos, because he had a Catholic wife and could not come to the Seder. I had already become so accustomed to such things among the ladder-climbing Jews in uniform that when occasionally a "Jewish officer," that is to say an officer who has not concealed his Jewishness, appeared, I found it truly surprising.

Once I traveled into Sendai, which lies in northern Japan. There I visited a large hospital where there lay Jewish soldiers, and where Jewish nurses were working. No sooner had I entered the doorway of the nicely appointed office to ask some information than a tall, handsome middle-aged lieutenant colonel came toward me, with a warm smile, gave me a strong, brotherly handshake, and cried out in pure Yiddish, "shalom aleichem, Chaplain! You have come to the right place and to the right man, I am Jewish."

I stood, simply stunned, but very pleased. This youthful officer quickly explained that he was the executive officer of the hospital and he would see to it that I could find the Jewish soldiers, doctors, and nurses. From my side, I told him I would like to arrange a Jewish service, and I had also brought along a movie about life in the state of Israel. My patron emitted a sound of joy, slapped me on the back and exclaimed, "Tonight we will have a Jewish evening!"

We did indeed have a Jewish evening. A lot of Jewish soldiers came to the hospital. They attentively followed the movie on the linen screen concerning the war in Israel. The service itself made a powerful impression. The Jewish colonel, himself, served hot coffee and refreshments, and there was "joy and happiness." We all spent the evening in a truly warm, Jewish manner.

The party lasted until quite late, and I had to hurry to the train in order to get back to Yokohama at the appointed time. I started packing my valise in haste, but the Colonel put me at ease. "What are you worried about? We will both go to Yokohama today." It turned out he needed to go to Yokohama by special hospital train. It was necessary to transport a number of patients to Tokyo. He promised me that on his order I would travel like a king. My companion did not exaggerate. We traveled, if not like kings, certainly as genuine counts. We had very nice, comfortable beds, a shower, hot and cold water. The service was excellent.

And so, sitting in the car together, the Colonel began to tell me his life history. His name was David Perloff. He was born in Lakishin,[10] near Minsk, in Russia in 1897. His father was a Hasidic Jew, with a long beard. He brought his children up with a strong Jewish spirit. When necessity brought him to America, he settled in Chicago. His wife and children had to remain in Russia for several years. After a few years, the father traveled back to his old home, to bring his family over to America, but while there, his wife died. For the sake of the children, he remarried and brought everyone to America.

In 1917, during the First World War, David Perloff went into the Army and served in Hawaii. A few years later he had risen to various higher ranks, and in 1942, he was an Army major. During the course of the Second World War, he acquired a post as assistant administrator to the chief surgeon in Teheran, Iran. He traveled all over the world and eventually became lieutenant colonel. He has been serving in the Army about thirty-three years. That is a considerable period in a man's life. He is, however, happy and cheerful. His son is a cadet at West Point, and before long he will graduate as an officer. It is a curious thing that he served in the First World War without citizenship papers. It was not until December 1918 that an Act of Congress declared that all aliens, foreign-born individuals who had served in the Army, could become American citizens. David Perloff, accordingly, became an American citizen without any preparation.

David Perloff told me these things about his personal life, while still in Japan, but when I came to Korea not long ago, to the Tenth Corps, whom did I meet here? The same, hearty David Perloff. He once again greeted me with a cordial, Jewish, "shalom aleichem," he, the lieutenant colonel from Sendai in Japan. Thereafter, we were together virtually everywhere, from Hungnam on, traveling together on the same ship. We both experienced the hell fire and the retreat. Now we are together by the coffee pot, speaking our beloved "mother-tongue," Yiddish.

When the conversation turned to the subject of Yiddish newspapers, he told me he is an avid reader of *Der Morgen Journal,* the newspaper that best represents how multifaceted is Jewish life in America. He is familiar with names of the writers for *Der Morgen Zhornal,* and since I am writing my articles for this newspaper, he asked me through my columns to send greetings to his brother and sisters who live in Los Angeles. The names are, Besse Poperny, Dora Simon, Ilene Goldfaden, Minetta Perloff, and Joseph Perloff, and in Chicago, he greets his brother Ben Perloff, and his sisters Ester Desner and Norma Levitan.[11]

Not long ago, David Perloff was awarded the Bronze Star for heroic action, when he fought and remained steadfast under enemy fire. He maintained his responsible position and did not leave until the very last minute, in spite of the hail of enemy fire overhead. I have purposely spoken extensively of David Perloff because he is an illustrious exception among those Jewish officers of high rank who do not take pride in their Jewishness. It is good to encounter, in various places, Jews who are proud of their people. Of all the journeys David Perloff has made throughout the world, no place made so deep an impression as the Jewish city of Tel Aviv. During the recent world war, he once went out for a walk through the streets of Tel Aviv and saw, from every window, and every house, light shining forth from the Sabbath candles. He had seen this great Jewish city immersed in the light of the Sabbath.

Such a scene can only be appreciated by a Jew who, although already thirty-three years in the Army and soon to be a full colonel, does not concede his Judaism. On the contrary, he bears his Jewish heritage like a badge of honor on his uniform.

Der Morgen Zhornal, March 11, 1951

Korea's Legendary Past and Her Present Reality

The Chinese Masters of Korea in a Previous Era

by Chaplain Milton J. Rosen

On one of my trips through Korea I met in the city of Kyongju a fifteen-year-old youngster, of whom it was said he is the smartest and most sophisticated boy in town—"the wise one of Kyongju."

Kyongju has a population of forty thousand inhabitants, and during the time I was there it seemed that just as many Koreans had come to tell me the history of their city. However, from all their tales I was not able to acquire a full picture . . . a story here, a story there, with only fragments emerging at the end. However, when the "wise one of Kyongju" invited me to his father's house to meet the members of his family, he let me know as an aside that he had a brother who was an instructor in history in the higher classes of the city's school. I was, indeed, most interested to meet this brother, in the hope I could get a full impression of Kyongju, the capital city of Shin-Ra, the pride of Korea.

In the small, modest house a kerosene lamp burned quite dimly, and the shadows chased one another across the wall in the glow of the battered lamp cylinder. The old farmer, a frail Korean with an aristocratic appearance, leisurely smoked a cigarette, half of which was contained in a long, brass tube. I offered his son, a handsome, refined boy of twenty-three, one of my cigarettes, but he politely refused since he did not smoke in the presence of his elderly father, a gesture of honor to the latter. The mother, also delicate, with a sensitive expression to her face, stood by silently, smiling.

It took quite some time before our conversation actually began. We just sat quietly and looked at one another. Suddenly, the father asked his younger son whether I am a Christian. "No, he is not a Christian," he replied. The father appeared relieved. It seemed that this old Korean was not enthralled with the Christians. He, himself, was a Buddhist and held that the missionaries in Korea were doing much damage. A Korean was a true Korean as long as he did not convert.

One word stimulates another. We spoke of religion and of politics until I became impatient and asked the teacher about the past history of the city. Apparently he had been waiting for the question and began, with great enthusiasm, to relate the history of Kyongju. He did not know a lot of English, but I was quite willing to listen to him in Japanese.

The Korean teacher prepared for his presentation as would a cantor his voice for his performance on the High Holidays. He blew his nose, wheezed, cleared his throat. By the time he was ready his father and mother were bursting with parental pride.

The first Koreans, my narrator related, were invaders from the large mass of land spreading out from the northeast portion of Asia. These people were driven by hunger and need. The poor fare did not suffice for the multitudinous population that consistently increased in numbers. These hungry people sought new land, new earth. At first they poured into the territory that today is known as Manchuria and is also quite populated.

Something of the history of this distant peninsula, Korea, can also be deduced from the stone handwork tools and from clay and earthen vessels that originate from a period some three thousand years ago. My narrator, the young teacher, poured forth words like a torrent. One could not stop his flowing language. I took the opportunity, as the mother shuffled out of the room, and the father began to doze, to ask the relator whether it was possible to acquire a book in English on the history of Korea. He assured me I would not be able to find even a single such book in the entire land. The Koreans burned all such books before the Communists invaded. Had the Communists found a book in English in a citizen's house, they would have shot the residents.[12]

Well, if there were no textbooks, one had to hear the story orally, and the facts, even from the mouth of my Japanese-speaking narrator, were quite remarkable. The first settlers on the peninsula were there 2,333 years before the Christian calendar, the leader of these people having been known as Tan Kon. These people existed independently about a thousand years. Thereafter, there appeared a Chinese warrior, Vi Man, from deep China. These soldiers invaded the land and conquered all of North Korea and named the state after their leader. However, their rule lasted only three generations. In the year 108 before the current Christian calendar, a Chinese king named Han established four colonies, that is, four separate small states, the best developed in North Korea, with its capital at Pyongyang. In more recent times, diggings in caves and caverns in various areas have unearthed treasures of gold, copper mirrors, and porcelain vessels. Indeed, in these dark caves have been found artistically painted pictures.

During the long Chinese occupation of North Korea, numerous kingdoms passed through. The most popular were the three Han dynasties, Man Han, Chin Han, and Bini Han. It was now getting late into the evening, and my narrator had not ceased relating facts and events that had played a role in the history of his land. His mother, reminding herself that one must extend hospitality to guests, brought in refreshments—hot green tea in small pots and, as an additional treat, salted fish. Here it must be mentioned that in Korea the richest refreshment one can offer an important guest is salted, dried fish. To my eyes, the fish appeared like blackened, thin sheets of paper. Just to look at it made me feel faint. The green tea was bearable, but merely the appearance of the dried fish was enough to drive one from Korea.

I tried to display politeness to my hostess. I quickly took a pot of horrendous looking tea and began to sip, but they kept pushing the fish toward me. I was much embarrassed. One could, perhaps, beg mercy from these good-hearted people, but in Korea there is no such mercy. When one honors you with refreshment, you must eat. You may not refuse. A black void passed before my eyes. Suddenly, a strange thought occurred to me. I asked my Korean friend if the fish had scales and fins.

He answered me in strong tones, "Certainly not!" He assured me firmly that these fish are fit for a king. I should not hesitate to eat them. I replied that a great doctor quite recently had forbidden me to eat fish, and especially fish without the above two characteristics.

My hosts were most ashamed. Their faces took on a deeper hue and they apologized. Thus I was saved from that most untempting fish, which I was sure would kill me. I do not exaggerate. The fish in Korea, a national dish, would have been for me a death sentence. One can see in the streets how adults and children walk around chewing pieces of dried fish, just as we in America chew chewing gum.

Meanwhile, my narrator, the teacher, had not relinquished his piece of Leviathan. He swallowed the piece of fish with great appetite. He was grinding with both cheeks, but when he was finished he continued for me his lecture on the history of Korea.

He told me about the various transformations through which his land had passed in the course of thousands of years and about the rulership that changed hands. He spoke of the foreign conquerors with disgust and of the nationalistic liberators with enthusiasm. He repeated tens of times the name of the great general Yul Chi Mondok, who, after many heavy battles against the invaders, freed his land. Even today, when one recalls the heroic general Mondok, one speaks of him in a spirit of great honor. He is renowned as a national liberator. The general's liberated country, however, did not enjoy a long existence. Other aggressors coveted Korea, but they did not succeed until the arrival of the "black day" in the year 668, when Korea fell into Chinese hands. The destitute Kingdom surrendered and the period of oppression and subjugation began

Notes

1. In 332 BCE, Alexander of Macedonia conquered the empire of Darius King of Persia, and with it 127 provinces, including that which was known as Palestine. The Greek culture, known as Hellenism among the nations under the aegis of Greek domination (including Babylon, Egypt, and Palestine), was generally well accepted in the area for nearly two centuries following the death of Alexander, until King Antiochus Epiphanes, a descendent of General Seleucus, who had conquered Babylon and Palestine under Alexander, came to the throne. Not content with the emphasis on physical beauty and other aspects of Hellenistic influence, Antiochus required his conquered subjects to adopt the worship of Greek gods and to accept all the Greek institutions including their dietary and social habits. Under this oppressive authority, sacrifices to Greek gods were offered up in the Holy Temple in Jerusalem, among others, and further sacrilege was perpetrated with the pouring of swine's blood upon the altar. These abominations were fiercely resisted, under the leadership of a local Hasmonean priest Matathius and his five sons, prominent among whom was the heroic fighter, Judah, known as the Maccabee, or hammer. On the plains of Emmaus, in 165 BCE, the vast armies of Antiochus were soundly defeated by a greatly outnumbered force under Judah, who then led his triumphant fighters to Jerusalem and the Temple, which was cleansed and rededicated. The Temple service required, among other things, the lighting of the Temple candelabrum with pure, undefiled oil. Tradition teaches that only enough pure oil was left to burn for one day, but the oil burned for eight days, until a new supply could be ready. For this reason, on the annual return of the Chanukah festival, the Jewish people all over the world use a candelabrum of eight candle or oil receptacles to burn a progressive number of lights, each night for eight nights.

2. The morning prayers, rendered daily by observant Jews, contain quotes from the Talmud regarding one's obligations to one's fellow man, as well as to religious study. These obligations, among which are those for which the religion prescribes no limits beyond the generosity of the giver, include acts of personal kindness and con-

sideration above those of general charity. "Bikur Cholim," visiting the sick, is one such deeply ingrained derivative of these precepts.

3. Yom Kippur. Day of Atonement. The annual observance, culminating the ten days of repentance that begin with Rosh Hashana, the Jewish New Year. A solemn day of fasting, prayer, and request for forgiveness of sins.

4. Kol Nidre. A solemn chant, offered on Yom Kippur eve, asking that any personal vows that might be made unknowingly or unwittingly during the coming year, which if not negated, could result in violating the sanctity with which Judaism regards a pledge, be considered null and void.

5. Mother's memorial. Refers to mother's "yahrzeit," the anniversary of her death. Among other religious observances, it is customary for the mourner, usually a son, to recite the "kaddish," a recognition of the power of the Almighty and praising of His name.

6. Shalom aleichem. A familiar form of greeting among Jewish people, meaning, in Hebrew, "Peace be unto you."

7. Presumably a reference to the story in Genesis, concerning the Chief Wine Steward, imprisoned by Pharaoh, whose dream predicting his restoration to his post was correctly interpreted by Joseph (Genesis XL).

8. Names and addresses transliterated from the Yiddish. Actual English spelling may vary from the transliterated versions.

9. Thirty-third Division?

10. Spelling uncertain.

11. All names transliterated. English spelling approximate.

12. It would appear that the dangers inherent in the reading of English texts aside, it would have been very difficult in March of 1951 to find an adequate history of Korea even in Japanese. Although a plethora of books on Korea, especially those in some way related to the Korean War, have appeared since, and very exhaustive histories are now available in English, this was not the case at the time of this conversation. It seems doubtful that any reference at the time would have offered Chaplain Rosen as fulfilling an experience relative to an understanding of Korea's development through the centuries as he might have obtained through the reading of Hatada Takashi's Chosen-shi (History of Korea). That history, published in Japanese in 1951, by a Japanese scholar, born in Korea in 1908, was unlikely to have been known to Chaplain Rosen or to his young lecturer. It was translated into English and published in English in 1969, by Warren W. Smith Jr. and Benjamin H. Hazard. (See bibliography.)

9

Japan Again

Chaplain Rosen had been in Korea for some ten months, when, sitting at breakfast with some other officers in Pusan, he was greeted by his medical officer with a direct order to appear in the clinic that afternoon for an examination. He had never registered any physical complaints at the clinic, with the exception of requiring crutches for a time because of a severely sprained right ankle, incurred when debarking from the ship on his return to Pusan from Hungnam. His schedule and circumstances, however, had been most taxing, due at least as much to his sense of mission on behalf of his Jewish flock as it was to the established duty of conducting services and counseling. The rigors of travel, not only with respect to troop movements, but also in terms of his constant trips by jeep to outlying units, in frigid cold or on dusty, rutted roads, the makeshift diet, exacerbated by his need to observe the restrictions relating to kosher food, and the inevitable uncertainties of military life and demands would ultimately have their effect on the unaccustomed middle-aged man. Added to this, the heavy load of seeking out and comforting the sick and wounded, ministering to the emotionally burdened, and worst of all, presiding at the burial services of the fallen, took its toll. He had not complained, however, and was shocked, at the end of his examination, to be told to pack up immediately for transfer to Japan. In Japan, he was taken to Osak Hospital, where, after surgery for bleeding hemorrhoids and time for recuperation, he recovered well.

Released in time for the High Holy Days of Rosh Hashana and Yom Kippur, he conducted services in Kobe at the Jewish synagogue built by the Sassoon family, before World War II. Thereafter, he was assigned to Camp Schimmelfennig, in northern Japan, where he requested a Jewish chapel. The latter was not practical, but he was given the use of a house, where he could provide kosher Sabbath meals and events related to religious-social customs, in addition to using the regular chapel for services. He was, at the time, the only Jewish chaplain in Japan. He traveled extensively to provide for Jewish troops in various parts of Japan, including flying to the northern island of Hokkaido to arrange for Passover services and the Passover Seder there. Before long, he received orders to reestablish his chaplain's duties in Yokohama, where he had originally founded the Jewish chapel. He was able to renew his old acquaintances there and expand the activities of the chapel, as he had on his first tour of duty. Even the staff was the same. The chapel once again became the center of Jewish life in Japan, with well-attended services, and a full social and cultural program. This worked particularly well for the Jewish troops coming to Japan on R&R leave from Korea.

The considerable number of Jewish servicemen coming to Japan on leave, generally arriving in Tokyo, was the impetus for negotiations that ultimately led to a new avenue for Chaplain Rosen's particular talents. A well-established Jewish Community Center (JCC) had been in existence for some time to cater to the needs of the Jewish expatriates from Russia and other European countries who had sought refuge in Japan over the years. There had, however, been very little association with representatives of the Jewish military personnel. At this time, however, it became evident to the Army as well as to representatives of the Jewish Welfare Board (JWB) in the United States, that the resources of the Center would be well employed on behalf of visiting soldiers and the community as a mutual meeting place and source of Jewish social and cultural life. For this purpose, a director was desirable and necessary, and when asked to fill this position, Chaplain Rosen, whose Army enlistment would soon be up, agreed to undertake the task. Following a brief return to the United States to undergo separation from the Army, he returned to Tokyo and began his years as director of the Jewish Welfare Board Armed Services Committee, with headquarters at the JCC. Following a gala opening, the center settled into a pleasant routine, which eventually accomplished the mixing of the civilian and military elements as it was conceived to do. Chaplain Rosen's job was to assist other chaplains in their planning and organization of programs and services, encompassing holidays, festivals and socials, and to provide at the Center a source of constant activity and a homelike atmosphere.

As a byproduct of this opportunity, a door opened that was to alter the emphasis of the rest of Chaplain Rosen's life. It began with his registration at the Naganuma Language School, where he undertook to study Japanese, graduating with honor and acquiring the capacity to carry on extensive conversations in the language and the ability to read simple Japanese. From this first insight into the culture that the language skills offered, a lifelong search was to begin. As he later wrote:

> This diploma gave me encouragement to start a new journey into Japanese life and culture. I was always puzzled by the people of the Far East. I felt I lived in a world half of which I understood and half of which I did not. As a Jew, I believed that all men think alike and act alike, and that only their language separates them. I found that it is not true at all. Language is not only different words, but different processes of thinking. Religions are not only different in belief, but also different in their concept of life, death, etc. I began to feel that I missed so much by not understanding the people of Japan, etc. I decided that when I am finished with this position, I would not go back to the rabbinate again in the States, but would come back to Japan and study the religions of the Orient, and in order to do that, to study in some Buddhist university, to learn the difference between Buddhism, Christianity, Judaism and Mohammedanism.

Consistent with the above, he did indeed immerse himself in study of the philosophies and languages of the East, and also found time to share his knowledge of Judaism with the many interested Japanese. He traveled throughout Japan, to speak to such groups as the Japan Israel Society and others, explaining to them, for the first time, the genuine essence of the religion, not for purposes of conversion, but for true, unsullied understanding. This had the result that when his term as director of the JWB in Tokyo came to its natural end, and it became necessary for him to leave Japan, there was considerable outcry among the Japanese. He continued to pursue his odyssey into the world of eastern thought and language elsewhere, but he had not left Japan forever.

Friday, April 6, 1956 THE NATIONAL JEWISH POST

Japanese Ask That Rabbi Milton J. Rosen Be Continued In Tokyo

● Editor, National Jewish Post

For the past few years when Rabbi Rosen served as chaplain in Japan and when he was recently the representative of the National Jewish Welfare Board in Tokyo at the Jewish Community Center, he has been a light and an inspiration to the Japanese people who had the privilege to meet him and enjoyed his personality and learning.

When his position with National Jewish Welfare Board terminated, we had heard that Rabbi Rosen was forced to leave Japan. We, the Japanese, especially the hundreds and perhaps thousands of people whom he had lectured and befriended, were so shocked and disappointed that even now feel the pain of forlornness. We have lost our guide and our true friend. He was to us the finest example of a Jew—wise, friendly, universal and willing to share with others his knowledge and also willing to learn our culture, customs and minds.

As busy as he was with his own work he took the pains to learn our language, which is one of the most difficult languages, in the world—if not the most difficult. He graduated from the famous Nagauma School of the Japanese Language. He studied diligently to read and write Japanese. He is doubtlessly the only rabbi in the world who can speak and converse in the Japanese.

HE LOVES the Japanese people with deep understanding and we respect him. He traveled many miles to cities, small towns and to distant islands where no westerner has ever been before at great sacrifice of his time and money and spoke the word of God—not to convert but to teach and learn.

He gave us such a great enlightenment of Judaism. His personality, his great heart, his deep mind as well as his humorous nature and his deep insight into the Japanese soul and above all his approachability and his humbleness made him incomparably admired by all of us in Japan who had met him.

How tragic that we lost him. How regrettable that he could not stay in Japan. Rabbi Rosen belongs in Japan. His abilities are wasted anywhere else. With over five million Jews in America one rabbi like Rabbi Rosen can not secure enough to establish a small Jewish-Japanese Culture Center in Japan. There are hundreds, if not thousands, who would seek to understand the great heritage of Israel.

ARE THERE any organizations in America who would help such a small project? Rabbi Rosen had never asked anything. He spent his own to spread the wisdom of Israel among the Japanese. We are sure that Rabbi Rosen will be satisfied to serve us if the organizations in America would only attempt to help him to establish such an oasis of Jewish culture in the great desert of spiritual emptiness in Japan. Judaism, we know however, is not pressing conversion—but the Jewish people should at least give the Japanese a chance to enjoy the cultural and philosophical aspects of its glorious heritage and give us a chance to see the other side of the fence—not only Christianity but also the mother of all the great religions—Judaism. If some wish to be converted—that would not be such a great loss either—maybe it would be an enrichment for Jewish life and prestige to the Jewish people.

WE APPEAL to you in the name of the great destiny of Israel and in the name of the glorious history of its people and great prophetic future to help us to promote and bring to a realization of our dream and hope which Rabbi Milton J. Rosen was so instrumental in creating—namely a Japanese-Jewish Culture Center in Japan.

The Christian Missions spend millions of dollars to spread their philosophy among the Japanese. A few thousand dollars a year will help to establish a Jewish-Japanese Culture Center.

Any small house where books and magazines and a few tables with Rabbi Rosen there to teach and befriend the Japanese will suffice as a beginning. Big buildings do not make a great center of learning—a small center with a great man like Rabbi Rosen will make a great and rich center. Is that a way to fulfill the purpose of great work Rabbi Rosen has undertaken?

We wish to thank the National Jewish Welfare Board who gave us the opportunity to enjoy Rabbi Rosen's radiant personality and his wisdom and friendliness during the past two years when he represented them in the Far East. When his position terminated here, also Japanese Culture Center activities terminated.

The time is short, the opportunity is here now, it may not come later if Rabbi Rosen really settles down in the United States.

Please respond to our urgent call.

Praying for your advice and help.

SHUICHIRO MATSUDA
2243, Kichijoji, Husashino-shi,
Tokyo, Japan

TAKESHI MATSUDA
SHIGEKO MIYAZAKI
TAKEKO MATSIN
FUKUINI SHIMURA
THEINI ONO
REIKO MITANI
EC IKENO
MR. & MRS. TADASHI SATO
AKISHISE TANAKO
TISHOHAGE TANAHO
VIYAKO SATO
HIROSHI MIYAZAWA
YOUICHI IIYAMA
KRIJIRO SHOMURA
PENZO SHIMURA
KUMIPO MIYAZAMA
KEISHI TANAKO
HIROMI YANAKA

Letter from the Japanese to the editor of the *National Jewish Post*

Epilogue

Chaplain Rosen had indeed not really left Japan. After spending a year as a teacher of Hebrew Studies in Chicago, he returned to Tokyo, where he was admitted to the University of Tokyo as a research fellow in the Faculty of Letters. By 1960, he had become a recognized and competent scholar in the Japanese language and in the reading of "Kambun," Japanese language of the ancient literature of Japanese Buddhism written in Chinese characters, and had acquired an outstanding capacity to understand and participate in literary discussions of a technical and philosophical nature, in Japanese. He had already begun working with UNESCO, a collaboration that included translating Japanese into English and that lasted until 1966. Also, in 1960 he was appointed to a research fellowship in World Jewish History through the Jewish University of America, taking up duties as a representative of the Faculty of the Jewish University of America in Japan. In addition to his formal studies at the university, he continued, after his official research appointment was over, to take informal guidance studies with prominent Japanese university professors, in Sanskrit, Indian philosophy, Buddhist philosophy, and the Pali language, and continued with great success in the reading of classical Chinese texts.

He traveled extensively during the next few years, ultimately continuing his formal courses at the School of Oriental and African Studies in London, from 1973 to 1976. Here, he deepened his understanding of Japanese Buddhism (studied in Japanese), Indian philosophy, and Sanskrit. He returned to the United States in the spring of 1976, in preparation for a sojourn in Taiwan, where he hoped to steep himself in the ancient Chinese disciplines. Apparently, as part of his application requirements, he outlined his reasons for wanting to study in Taiwan.

> During my chaplaincy in the US Army, stationed in Japan and later in Korea, I took advantage of the opportunity to meet priests and intellectuals of the various Buddhist Mahayana sects of the Far East. Having been impressed by the philosophical concepts and the humanitarian aspects of Buddhism, I began to study the Japanese language. While still in the Army, I finished a course in Elementary Japanese Conversation. When my service in the Army terminated, I returned to Japan, after having been accepted as a research fellow on the Faculty of Letters at Tokyo University, and ardently pursued the courses offered in the Department of Indian Philosophy. During that time, I also got a diploma from the Naganuma Japanese Language School in Tokyo.
>
> After having spent several years in studying Buddhist books written in "Kanbun" (Chinese characters read in Japanese), I suddenly realized how important it was to acquire a knowledge of the Chinese language, in order to gain a deeper insight into the original meaning of the content of these books and manuscripts, especially those which were originally written in Chinese. I therefore resolved to study Chinese when the opportunity presented itself. I had heard about London University and its Department of Oriental and African Studies. I applied for entrance and was accepted. I was advised by the faculty of that department that before I become deeply involved in Chinese studies, I should try to get some knowledge in basic Sanskrit. I followed this advice and studied Sanskrit for several terms. After that, I began to study Chinese, particularly classical Chinese, for several terms. My interest in this field is very intense and will not be satisfied unless I find the school and place where I am able to become completely immersed in an atmosphere that is all Chinese. Therefore, teachers of Chinese and students who study in the Republic of China periodically, in order to enhance their Chinese, have advised me to choose the Republic of China as the ideal place to make my dream come true.
>
> My purpose in all this is to enrich myself with such knowledge as to enable me to pursue a work on comparative religious thought processes of the East and West, which I hope to contribute in the future.

The dream was not to be realized. On June 25, 1976, Milton Rosen suffered a fatal heart attack. With his death, a light was extinguished, and with that light, the potential for a deep and unique insight into the human condition.

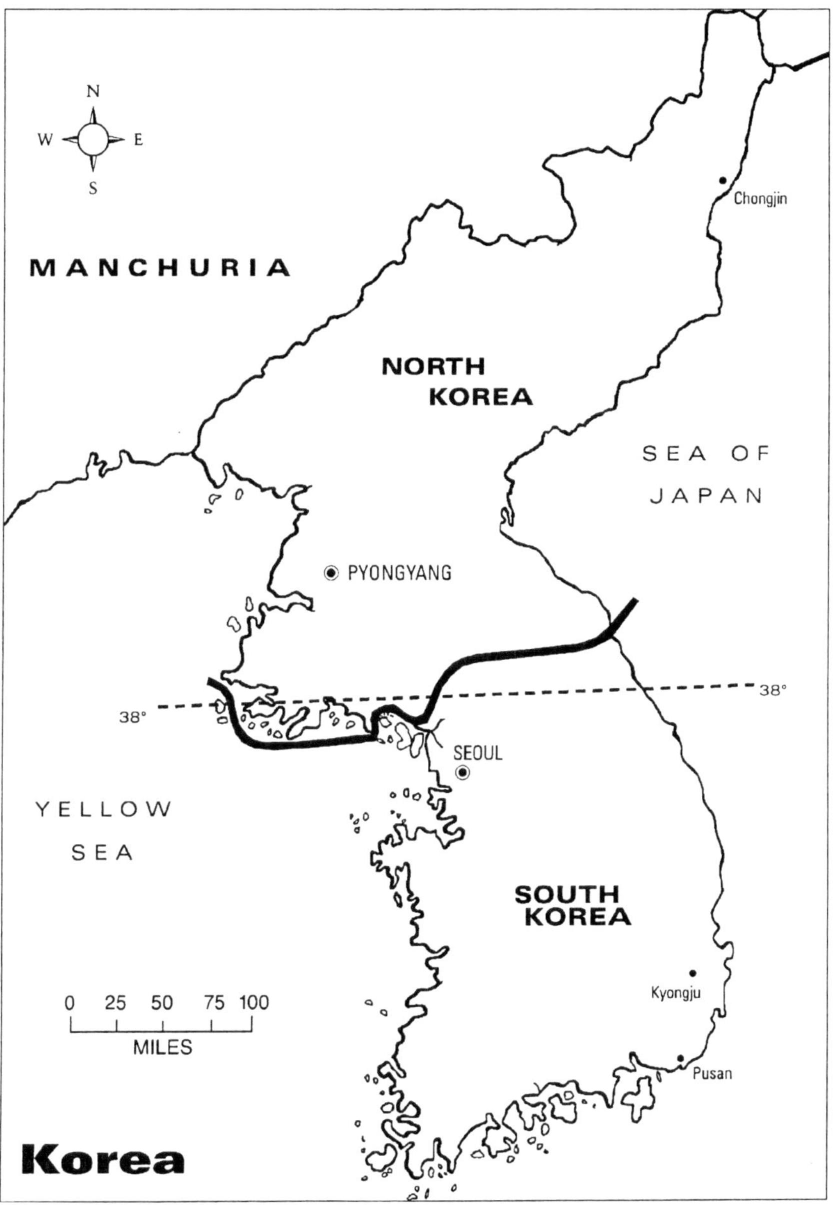

Cease-Fire Line.

Bibliography

Encyclopedia Judaica, *Jewish Morning Journal.* Jerusalem: Keter Publishing House Ltd., 1975.

Hickey, Michael. *The Korean War: The West Confronts Communism, 1950–1953.* Woodstock, N.Y.: Overlook Press, 1999.

Insight Guide: Korea. Englewood Cliffs, N.J.: APA Productions, 2001.

Kaufman, Burton. *The Korean Conflict.* Westport, Conn.: Greenwood Press, 1999.

Kim Chun Kon. *The Korean War, 1950–1953.* Seoul, Korea: Kwangmyong Publishing Co. Ltd., 1973.

MacDonald, Callum A. *Korea: The War before Vietnam.* New York: Free Press, 1987.

Nilsen, Robert. *South Korea Handbook.* Hong Kong: Moon Publications, 1977.

Passow, David. *The Prime of Yiddish.* Jerusalem: Gefen, 1996.

Rosen, Jeffrey Solomon. *The Korean War.* Unpublished manuscript. 1975.

Russ, Martin. *The Last Parallel: A Marine's War Journal.* New York: Fromm International Publishing, 1977.

Savada, Andrea Matles, and William Shaw. *South Korea: A Country Study.* Washington, D.C.: Federal Research Division, Library of Congress, 1992.

Stokesbury, James L. *A Short History of the Korean War.* New York: William Morrow, 1988.

Takashi Hatada. *A History of Korea.* Santa Barbara, Calif.: ABC-CLIO, 1969.

Index

Adam, Walter H., 98
Alexander of Macedonia, 111n. 1
Almond, Gen. Edmond, 20, 22, 24, 39, 77
American Air Force, 39, 49, 50, 58
American Far East Policy, 2
American Jewish Periodical Center, xvi
Antiochus IV Epiphanes, 111n. 1
Anti-Semite, 54
Anti-Semites, 32

Bathhouse, Pusan, 72–73
Bazookas, 18
Bar mitzvah, 63
Behr, John, 98
Bikur Cholim, 87, 111n. 2
Bolsheviks, 3
Borak, Lt. Emanuel, 98
British soldiers, 36, 38n. 4
Buddhism, 115, 117, 118
Buddhist, 108, 115, 118

Cairo Conference, 1, 2, 5
Camp Schimmelfennig (Japan), 114
Canadian soldiers, 36,
Chanukah, 87, 89, 111n. 1
Chaplain Rosen. *See* Rosen, Chaplain Milton J.
Chaya Basha, 11
Chiang Kai-shek, 2–5
Chinanpo, 40
Chinese Civil War, 2–5
Chinese classical texts, 117, 118
Chinese Communists, 2–4, 55, 60, 65, 66, 68, 72
Chinese invasion of North Korea, 22, 24, 39, 40
Chipyong-ni, 66
Chonan, 18
Chongchon River, 22, 39
Chosen Reservoir, 24, 33, 39, 103
Chou En-lai, 4
Christian missionaries, 54
Christian officers, 104
Chu Te, 4
Chunchon, 15
Churchill, Winston, 2
Coalition government, Communist Chinese and Kuomintang presiding jointly over China, 4
Cohen, Harry, 57
Commonwealth troops, 38n. 4, 39, 65
Communist Party, 3
Cooper, Professor, 55
Council of Foreign Ministers, 7

Daily Bulletin. *See* Tageblat
Dean, Gen. William F., 18, 19
Democratic People's Republic of Korea, 8

Der Morgen Zhornal (*Jewish Morning Journal*), xv, 13, 24, 25, 29, 33, 41, 45, 49, 53, 56, 57, 67, 71, 79, 83, 87, 88, 91, 96, 100, 104, 107, 108
Der Tog (The Day), 13
Dewey, John, 28
Diskin Orphanage, 10
Djerling, Saul, 98

Eighth Army. *See* US Eighth Army
Eisenberg, Stanley, 98
Emmaus, Battle of, 111n. 1
Empire of Japan, 1
Europe, eastern, 13

Far Eastern Command. *See* US Far Eastern Command
Fifth Regimental Combat team. *See* US Fifth Regimental Combat team
Finkelstein, Jerry, 57
First Calvary Division. *See* US First Calvary Division
First Marine Division. *See* US First Marine Division
First Provisional Marine Brigade. *See* US First Provisional Marine Brigade
Fort Bragg, NC, 11
Forverts (Forward), 13
Forward. *See* Forverts
Four States. *See* Han Dynasty

General Haase, troopship, 25
German Jews, 12
Germany, 1
Germany, Nazi, 12
Goldberg, N., 98
Goldman, Cpl. Allen P., 98
Goodman, Chaplain Garson, 89, 99
Great Britain, 1, 2
Guerilla camps, 30

Hatada, Takashi (*History of Korea*), 112n. 12
Hagaru, 40
Hamhung, 33, 39–42, 56, 72, 85, 87
Han Dynasty (Four States), 109
Han River, 7
Harbin, 55
Harrison High School, 10
Hebrew Pre-Theological College of Chicago, 10
Hebrew Theological College of Chicago, 10
Hellenism, 111n. 1
Hing Bang Hok, Dr., 53–55
Hiroshima, 5
Hodge, Lt. Gen. John R., 6, 7
Hokkaido, 114
Houseboy(s), 28, 33, 35
Hungnam, 12, 32, 40–43, 45, 54, 56, 57, 69–72, 78, 79, 107, 113

Inchon, 20, 22, 24, 25, 27, 30, 35, 40
Indian philosophy, 117, 118
Indian soldiers, 36
Inflation, South Korea, 74
Interim People's Committee, N. Korea, 8
Israel, State of, 28
Iwon, 22, 24

Japan, xvi, 1, 2, 5, 11, 12, 19, 24, 25, 45, 51, 67, 83, 93, 104, 113–115, 117, 118
Japanese Constitution, 11
Japan-Israel Society, 12, 115
Jerusalem, 10
Jewish Chapel Center, Tokyo, 12, 62, 63
Jewish Community Center, Tokyo, 114, 116
Jewish Journal and Daily News. *See* Der Morgen Zhornal
Jewish Morning Journal. *See* Der Morgen Journal
Jewish University of America, 117
Jewish War of Liberation, 87
Jewish Welfare Board, 57, 114, 115, 116
Joint Chiefs of Staff. *See* US Joint Chiefs of Staff
Judah Maccabee, 111n. 1
Judaism, 12, 83–85, 115,
Juichin, 4

Kaesong, 15, 18
Kaftan, 26
Kambun, 117, 118
Kiangsi Province, 3
Kiddush, 52
Kim Il Sung, 8

Kobe, Jewish synagogue in, 114
Koltof, Capt. Sheldon, 98
Kook, Chief Rabbi (of Israel), 10
Korean independence, 2, 6, 7
Korean Military Advisory Group (KMAG), 8, 17
Korean People's Army, 9
Korean People's Republic, 9
Koto-ri, 39
Kum River, 19
Kunu-ri, 39
Kuomintang (Nationalist Party), 3, 4, 5
Kyongju, 65, 75, 85, 108, 109

Land reform, North korea, 8
L'chaim, 84, 103
Letter from the Japanese, 116
Levitas, Capt. Stanley D., 98
Lipchitz, Chaplain Oscar M., 99
L.S.T.'s, 36

Maariv, 98
Mac Arthur, Gen. Douglas, 15, 18, 20, 22, 38, 66
Maccabee. *See* Judah Maccabee
Madison, Wisconsin, 11
Manchu Dynasty, 3
Manchuria, 2, 3, 5, 20
Mao Tse-tung, 3–5
Margolin, Oliver, 103
Marshall, Gen. George C., 5
Marxist model of government, 3
Massacre of Communists in Shang-hai, 3
Mattathias, 111n. 1
Matzos, 57, 60, 84–86, 98, 104, 105
Messing, Chaplain Joseph B., 99
Mincha, 98
Mohammedanism, 115
Mondok, Yul Chi, 111
Mongolia, Outer, 2

Naktong River, 28
Naganuma Language School, 115, 118
Nagasaki, 5, 6
National Assembly, South Korea, 7
Nationalist Party. *See* Kuomintang
Nationwide elections, Korea, 7
Ninth Corps (IX Corps). *See* US IX Corps
North Korea, 5–9, 29
North Korean Communists, 7, 55
North Korean Divisions (Second, Third, Fifth, and Sixth), 19
North Korean Infantry, 18
North Korean Invasion of South Korea, 15
North Korean 105th Armored Division, 19

Okinawa, 6
Oksan, 93, 95
Ongjin Peninsula, 3
Operation Killer, 66
Osan, 18

Palestine, 10
Pali language, 117
People's Executive Committee, North Korea, 6
Perloff, Lt. Col. David, 105–107
Phylacteries, 89
Potsdam Conference, 2, 3, 5
Protestant, 32
Pusan, 18, 29, 30, 33–36, 38n. 1, 65, 69, 71–73, 79–81, 113
Pyongtek, 18
Pyongyang, 8, 12, 39

Republic of China, 2
Republic of Korea, 15. *See* ROK
Reznick, Nathan David, 88
Rhee, Syngman, 7
Ridgeway, Lt. Gen. Matthew, 65, 66
Rock of Ages, 89
Rocket launchers, 3.5 inch, 19
ROK, 40
ROK I Corps, 20, 22, 65
ROK First Division, 21, 39
ROK II Corps, 20, 22, 39, 65
ROK Seventh Division, 15
ROK Sixth Division, 32
Ronnel, Joseph, 98
Roosevelt, Franklin, 2–5
Rosen, Chaplain Milton J., 10–12, 14, 24, 33, 38, 43, 44, 61–65, 88, 113–118
Rosh Hashana, 113
Russia, 1, 2, 114

Russian Jews, 12
Russian Twenty-fifth Army, 6
Russo-Japanese War of 1904, 2, 26

Sabbath, 11, 60, 84
Sanskrit, 117, 118
Sarah, 11
Sasebo, 25
Sassoon, family of, 114
Sayings of the Fathers, 89
Schimmelfenning. *See* Camp Schimmelfennig
Schlesinger, Ralph, 98
School of Oriental and African Studies, London, 117, 118
Sea of Japan, 1
Second Infantry Division. *See* US Second Infantry Division
Seidenberg, Isador, 98
Seleucus, Gen., 111n. 1
Sendai, 105
Seoul, 15, 17, 20, 25, 34, 65
Seventh Infantry Division. *See* US Seventh Infantry Division
Shabsai, 10, 11
Shang-hai massacre, 3
Shensi Province, 4
Shalom aleichem, 94, 106, 112n. 6
Silberman, Abe, 57, 86
Smith, Lt. Col. Charles B., 18
Smith, Gen. Oliver, USMC, 40
South Korea, 7, 8, 12, 17, 24
Soviet Union, 3, 17
Stalin, Joseph, 3, 75
Stars and Stripes, 75
Sun Yat-sen, 3
Support units, 65
Supreme People's Assembly, North Korea, 8

Taejon, 18, 19
Tageblat (Daily Bulletin), 13
Taiwan, 5, 117
Talmud, 10, 85
Tan Kon, 109
Tanks, T-34, 17, 18
Task Force Smith, 18
Tel Aviv, 107
Tenth Corps (X Corps). *See* US X Corps
The Day. *See* Der Tog
38th Parallel, 6, 15, 18, 20, 39, 66
Toby, Col. (Chief Chaplain, US X Corps), 42, 56, 78
Tokyo, 15, 114–118
Torah, 10, 89
Truman, Harry, 2, 5, 7, 12, 32, 41, 78
Trusteeship, four-power, 2, 7
Turkish units, 65

United Nations, 5, 17, 28, 50, 71
UNESCO, 117
UN Security Council, 17
UN Temporary Commission, Korea, 7
United States, 1, 2, 5, 7, 8, 17, 18
US Eighth Army, 18, 39
US Far East Command, Japan, 18
US Fifth Regimental Combat Team, 19
US First Calvary Division, 19
US First Marine Division, 20, 24, 39, 44, 49
US First Provisional Marine Brigade, 19
US I Corps, 20, 65
US Joint Chiefs of Staff, 22
US IX Corps, 65
US occupation of Japan, 11
US Second Infantry Division, 39
US Seventh Infantry Division, 20, 24, 39, 40, 43, 45, 98, 103
US X Corps, 20, 22, 24, 29, 39, 43, 45, 65, 106
US Twenty-fifth Infantry Division, 19
US Twenty-fourth Infantry Division, 18, 19
University of Seoul, 28, 53
University of Tokyo, Faculty of Letters, 117, 118
University of Wisconsin, 11
Unsan, 24

Van Fleet, Gen. James, 66
Vilna, 10
Vi Man, 109

Wake Island: Meeting between Pres. Truman and Gen. Mac Arthur (October 15, 1950), 22
Walker, Lt. Gen. Walton, 18, 19, 65
Wise One of Kyongju, 108

Won, 31, 32, 74
Wonsan, 22, 29, 34, 36
World War I, 10, 106
World War II, 1, 106

Yahrzeit, 111n. 5
Yalta, 2
Yalu River, 20, 22, 24, 40, 76
Yangtze River, 4
Yellow Sea, 1
Yenan, 4
Yiddish, xv, xvi, 10, 13, 14, 24, 88, 93, 94, 97
Yokohama, 11, 62, 63, 106, 114
Yom Kippur, 93, 94, 113
Yudam-ni, 39, 40

About the Editor

Born in Oklahoma City, Stanley Rosen passed his childhood years in the southern United States. He eventually moved to Chicago, where he studied at the Hebrew Theological College for several years and received a B.A. degree from Roosevelt University in 1951. Following his graduation and marriage, he lived nearly a year in Israel, exploring kibbutz life for a time, before taking residence in Jerusalem, where he wrote a radio script on the lighter side of life in Israel, broadcasting regularly to Great Britain through Radio Kol Tzion Lagola (Voice of Zion to the Diaspora).

He served in the United States Army from 1953 to 1955, fourteen months of which were spent in Korea, where he was assigned to the IX Corps Public Information Office. His tour was devoted in large measure to writing feature articles for *Army Times* and *Stars and Stripes,* recording and announcing VIP and other events of interest, and interviewing troops for hometown radio station rebroadcast.

On his return to the United States, he taught private school for a number of years while taking premedical courses part time, eventually graduating from medical school at the University of Zurich, with the help of the G.I. Bill. He practiced internal medicine in Illinois and Wisconsin for thirty years before retiring in the mid-1990s. He lives with his wife, Bernice, in Evergreen, Colorado. He has a daughter, Lynn, and three grandchildren, Jay, Sharon, and Rebecca.